Mark Twain's Escape from

Mark Twain's *Escape from Time*

A Study of Patterns and Images

Susan K. Harris

University of Missouri Press

Columbia & London, 1982

Copyright © 1982 by
The Curators of the University of Missouri
Library of Congress Catalog Card Number 82–1981
Printed and bound in the United States of America
University of Missouri Press, Columbia, Missouri 65211

Library of Congress Cataloging in Publication Data

Harris, Susan K., 1945–
    Mark Twain's Escape from Time.

    Bibliography: p. 161
    Includes index.
    1. Twain, Mark, 1835–1910—Philosophy.
2. Twain, Mark, 1835–1910—Religion and ethics.
I. Title.
PS1337.3.H37   818'.409   82–1981
ISBN 0–8262–0369–8   AACR2

Chapter 1 appeared in slightly different form in the *Journal of Narrative Technique* 12, no. 1 (Winter 1982).
Parts of chapters 5 and 8 appeared in different form in *Essays in Literature* 7, no. 2 (Fall 1980).

*To Billy, my husband,
and
To Don, my friend*

Acknowledgments

Perhaps the most memorable aspect of my experience in writing this book has been the almost universal kindness shown me by the scholars and editors I have contacted in regard to it. When I first appeared at the Mark Twain Papers at Berkeley in the summer of 1978, the late Fred Anderson, then General Editor of the Papers, became the first person to encourage my project. During the summers of 1979 and 1980, Dahlia Armon and other staff members extended every possible help and courtesy to me. Without access to the Papers some of the most interesting parts of this book would not have been written, and without the permission of the Mark Twain Foundation, those parts would not have been published. All previously unpublished materials by Mark Twain quoted here are copyrighted 1982 by the Mark Twain Foundation and published with the permission of the University of California Press and the General Editor of the Mark Twain Project, Robert H. Hirst; all previously unpublished material is cited as such in my footnotes. My thanks go to all the dedicated members of the Mark Twain Project.

Others have been generous of their time and unstinting of their help. Professor Henry Nash Smith was kind enough to meet and talk with me that first summer at Berkeley and to read the successive drafts of the manuscript that I sent him. Any merits of rigor or style the book may possess are likely to be the results of his urging; any defects are entirely my own. My colleague Donald D. Stone was equally munificent, not only reading the manuscript for logic and content but also suggesting revisions of specific lines for syntax and clarity. Together, Henry Nash Smith and Donald D. Stone have taught me what the concept of generosity truly means. H. Daniel Peck, Charles H. Molesworth, and David H. Richter also read the manuscript in whole or part, and their comments helped me determine my direction. The members of the Queens College Liberal Arts Faculty Seminar, especially Edith Wyschogrod, Hilail Gildin, Joseph Carpino, Nino Langiulli, Jean Fontinell, and Louis Finkelstein, all influenced the book through their lively discussions of philosophical—especially phenomenological—ideas. Finally, not only Henry Nash Smith but also David Levin, Richard Slotkin, and Sacvan Bercovitch all encouraged and helped me during the tense period before the book's acceptance for publication; to all these gracious scholars, I owe my deepest gratitude.

This research was supported in part by a grant from the City University of New York PSC-BHE Research Award Program; in addition the Queens College Faculty-in-Residence Awards Program enabled me to complete the manuscript in the Fall of 1980 by granting me released time.

That my first and last obligations are to William J. Harris goes without saying; to him I owe not just my gratitude, but all my love.

S.K.H.
Brooklyn, N.Y.
30 March 1982

Contents

Short References

"A&E" — "Adam's Diary" and "Eve's Diaries." In *The $30,000 Bequest. The Complete Works of Mark Twain*, 18:342–81. New York: Harper and Brothers, 1917.

"AKS" — "About All Kinds of Ships." In *In Defense of Harriet Shelley, The Complete Works of Mark Twain*, 16:288–312. New York: Harper and Brothers, 1925.

CY — *A Connecticut Yankee in King Arthur's Court.* San Francisco: Chandler Publishing Co., 1963.

"CYS" — "The Chronicle of Young Satan." In *Mark Twain's Mysterious Stranger Manuscripts*, edited by William M. Gibson, pp. 35–174. Berkeley: University of California Press, 1969.

"FCCC" — "The Facts Concerning the Recent Carnival of Crime in Connecticut." In *Great Short Works of Mark Twain*, edited by Justin Kaplan, pp. 113–28. New York: Harper and Row, 1967.

FE — *Following the Equator.* In *The Complete Travel Books of MT*, edited by Charles Neider, 2:667–1084. Garden City, N.Y.: Doubleday and Co., 1967.

"No. 44,MS" — "No. 44, The Mysterious Stranger." In *Mark Twain's Mysterious Stranger Manuscripts*, edited by William M. Gibson, pp. 221–405. Berkeley: University of California Press, 1969.

"GD" — "The Great Dark." In *Mark Twain's Which Was the Dream? and Other Symbolic Writings of the Later Years*, edited by John S. Tuckey, pp. 102–50. Berkeley: University of California Press, 1966.

HF — *Adventures of Huckleberry Finn*, edited by Henry Nash Smith. Boston: Houghton Mifflin, Riverside Editions, 1958.

"HTI" — "Huck Finn and Tom Sawyer Among the Indians." In *Mark Twain's Hannibal, Huck and Tom*, edited by Walter Blair, pp. 81–140. Berkeley: University of California Press, 1969.

IA — *The Innocents Abroad.* New York: New American Library, Signet edition.

JA — *Personal Recollections of Joan of Arc by The Sieur Louis de Conte.* 2 vols. New York: Harper and Brothers, 1899.

"LE" — "Letters from the Earth." In *Letters from the Earth*, edited by Bernard DeVoto, pp. 11–25. New York: Harper and Row, 1962.

LM — *Life on the Mississippi*. New York: New American Library, 1961.

"MPS" — "My Platonic Sweetheart." In *The Mysterious Stranger and Other Stories*, pp. 287–304. New York: Gabriel Wells, 1923.

P&P — *The Prince and The Pauper*. New York: New American Library, 1964.

RI — *Roughing It*. In *The Complete Travel Books of MT*, edited by Charles Neider, 1:436–806. Garden City, N.Y.: Doubleday & Co., 1966.

"3,000 Years" — "Three Thousand Years Among the Microbes." In *Mark Twain's Which Was the Dream? and Other Symbolic Writings of the Later Years*, edited by John S. Tuckey, pp. 433–553. Berkeley: University of California Press, 1966.

TA — *A Tramp Abroad*, edited by Charles Neider. New York: Harper and Row, 1977.

TS — *The Adventures of Tom Sawyer*. New York: New American Library, 1959.

WM — *What Is Man?* New York: Harper and Brothers, 1917.

"WW" — "In a Writer's Workshop." In *Mark Twain in Eruption*, edited by Bernard DeVoto, pp. 196–201. New York: Harper and Brothers, 1922.

"WWD" — "Which Was the Dream?" In *Mark Twain's Which Was the Dream? and Other Symbolic Writings of the Later Years*, edited by John S. Tuckey, pp. 33–73. Berkeley: University of California Press, 1966.

"WWI" — "Which Was It?" In *Mark Twain's Which Was the Dream? and Other Symbolic Writings of the Later Years*, edited by John S. Tuckey, pp. 179–429. Berkeley: University of California Press, 1966.

Introduction

In 1865, claiming that he had had "but two *powerful* ambitions in my life"—to be a riverboat pilot and a "preacher of the Gospel"—Sam Clemens "renounced" the latter in a letter to his brother Orion, declaring, instead,

> I *have* had a 'call' to literature, of a low order—i.e., humorous. It is nothing to be proud of, but it is my strongest suit, and if I were to listen to that maxim of stern *duty* which says that to do right you *must* multiply the one or the two or the three talents which the Almighty entrusts to your keeping, I would long ago have ceased to meddle with things for which I was by nature unfitted and turned my attention to seriously scribbling to excite the *laughter* of God's creatures.[1]

Clemens's letter is not altogether serious—as James M. Cox notes in *Mark Twain: The Fate of Humor*, its pomposity signals Twain's comic hyperbole[2]—but Clemens's rationale, his contention that his call to preach was only undermined by his lack of the requisite religious devotion, accurately describes his dilemma. Impatient of, and often annoyed by, religious dogma, Sam Clemens still possessed enough moral energy to have sustained several average ministers. The pulpit would have

---

1. *Mark Twain's Notebooks and Journals*, vol. 1, 1855–1873, edited by Frederick Anderson, Michael B. Frank, and Kenneth Sanderson, p. 92. Twain's emphasis.
2. James M. Cox, *Mark Twain: The Fate of Humor*, pp. 32–33. Mark Twain's humor has been amply treated in critical literature. Not only Cox but also Kenneth S. Lynn, in *Mark Twain and Southwest Humor* (Boston: Little, Brown & Co., 1959); Franklin R. Rogers, in *Mark Twain's Burlesque Patterns, as Seen in the Novels and Narratives, 1855–85* (Dallas: Southern Methodist University Press, 1960); Pascal Covici, Jr., in *Mark Twain's Humor: The Image of a World;* and, more recently, David E. E. Sloane, in *Mark Twain Comedian,* have written full-length studies, and Mark Twain's humor is always treated in general studies such as Constance Rourke's classic *American Humor: A Study of the National Character* (Garden City, N.Y.: Doubleday, 1931), Walter Blair's *Native American Humor* (San Francisco: Chandler Publications, 1937), and Tony Tanner's *The Reign of Wonder* (Cambridge: Cambridge University Press, 1966). In addition it is studied in any work examining Twain's style, such as Henry Nash Smith's *Mark Twain: The Development of a Writer* and William Gibson's *The Art of Mark Twain*. Despite the attention that I—and many other recent

1

been an appropriate place for him to castigate the inadequacies of the world.

Despite his attention to "laughter," the moral impulse that had tempted Sam Clemens to "meddle" did not vanish from Mark Twain's work. Far from disappearing into his lowest humor, it manifested itself in his highest, transmuting his critique of human nature into witticisms that provoke reflection rather than homilies that stultify it. The didactic Twain can be seen in his attacks on hypocrisy and convention; even his Western sketches often poke fun at idealists who cling to their dreams at the expense of their responsibilities.[3] Nevertheless, Twain's early vision implies that human beings are funny because they are fallible—and therefore capable of improvement—rather than, like Jonathan Swift's more bilious belief, that they are amusing because they are vile. Yet even Twain's apprentice satires share Swift's moral intentions, and his wit, though generous, is deftly aimed. His aphorisms, for instance, are pointed: they savage our pretensions. Similarly, the irony with which many of his characters attack the weaknesses in others, or in themselves, reveals a Calvinist sense of depravity. Even the early Mark Twain is haunted by the suspicion that human foibles should really be called sins, and, as readers of his dark writings know, when his faith in moral perfectionism ceased to sustain him, his buoyancy deserted him and invective assumed a major role in his writing.[4] Certainly there is a marked change in the quality of his later work; not only do his efforts to

critics—pay to Twain's "dark writings," his humor remains, of course, the "real" reason we read Mark Twain.

3. Cox, *The Fate of Humor*, p. 12.

4. The "other" side of Mark Twain's humor—his anger, his moralism, his pessimism—has always been recognized and has been a subject of critical controversy since publication of Van Wyck Brooks's *The Ordeal of Mark Twain* (New York: E. P. Dutton & Co., 1920). Typical of the controversy is the tendency to look at Samuel Clemens's pseudonym as expressing the dual aspect of his nature: his explosions of anger and his eruptions of mirth seem different manifestations of the same response. In recent years attention has tended to focus on Twain's late life and "dark" writings, for example, Hamlin Hill's study of Twain's last decade, *Mark Twain: God's Fool*, and Sholom J. Kahn's study of the *Mysterious Stranger* manuscript texts; and specific attention to Twain's humorous writings has become less prominent. Increasingly, Twain is seen within the context of late-nineteenth-century frustrations and disappointments

be funny fail, but in the manuscripts left unfinished during his last decade, in large sections of published works (such as *Pudd'nhead Wilson*, 1894) prior to that, and, of course, in protest essays such as "The United States of Lyncherdom," he ceased even attempting to provoke laughter. Rather, the preacher in Mark Twain unmasked himself and openly attacked his congregation's moral failings. Moreover, in works like *What Is Man?* he even turned to metaphysics, revealing a determination to approach the issues from a serious philosophical point of view. Thus, although humor and satire are always alternatives in Twain's writings, their relative weights shift over the years: humor dominates his earlier work; increasingly bitter satire his later.

Rather than treating the way Mark Twain's humor and satire alternate to disguise or reveal his moral frustrations, however, this study utilizes Gaston Bachelard's concept of "preferred images"—images that give unity to a writer's imaginative world—to examine the way Mark Twain's lyrical modes furnished him with a third alternative: an imaginative escape from despair. In addition to using laughter and invective to attack human errors, Mark Twain used images of water, space, childhood, and women to escape the psychological loneliness his emotional response to moral issues inspired. Generally embedded in the most lyrical passages in any given work, and frequently imbued with a degree of sentimentality offensive to modern readers, these images resonate with the "peace," "tranquillity," and "contentment" that neither Twain nor the characters who reflect his sense of alienation seemed able to obtain in ordinary life. In his writings they operate as images of repose to which both he and his narrative personae gravitate for respite when their own pain, or their perceptions of the pain of others, threatens to overwhelm them.

Even though this work begins with an examination of narrative alienation, it is primarily a study of those recurring images that serve to *resolve* alienation in Mark Twain's writings. I hope to show that the patterns of alienation and resolution identified by these images anticipate the philosophy of mind Mark Twain

---

over the fact that man's moral development had not kept pace with his technological advances.

developed in his later years. While it is easy to dismiss Twain's contentions, from the late 1890s on, that he had a *"spiritualized self* which can *detach itself* and go wandering off upon affairs of its own" as simply evincing his wish to escape his personal turmoil, we should not dismiss the fact that he believed that self to be immune to human anguish and free of temporal restrictions. In reading Twain's later writings I was struck by the images he used to illustrate these ideas; all of these images also occur in earlier works, and all serve as antidotes to anxieties engendered by both his personal tragedies and the sight of other people's pain. By studying the patterns in which the images occur—that is, what particular ones suggest to the narrator and how they function within the narrative plot—I became conscious of the consistency with which these images help relieve the narrator's tensions by presenting him with an ideal otherworld in which human suffering is no longer inevitable. Unlike Mark Twain's determinism, which reveals his frustration about the cause-and-effect universe, the philosophy of mind these images suggest reveals the joyousness with which he viewed the possibility of escape from time. They signal steps in the slow evolution of a theory that his creative consciousness might be capable of transcending human time and thus escaping the determinist trap.

It is important to note that in this study the term *alienation* does not refer to existential alienation, the alienation typified by Camus's Stranger, who was so deadened to the world as to be incapable of emotional response. Rather, the term refers to a moral alienation that manifests itself psychologically. Both Mark Twain and his narrative personae, far from being deadened to the world, are deeply, passionately, alive to it. Alienation is an aspect of their response; the term describes their sense of being psychological outsiders, characters who never feel wholly, that is, unselfconsciously, part of their own societies. This does not mean that Mark Twain's alienated characters do not function effectively—even happily—in their social environment. Nevertheless, they are sufficiently at odds with some significant aspect of prevailing belief that they never participate wholeheartedly in the *geist*, or spirit, of their time. In *Mark Twain and the Community*, Thomas Blues interprets this strain as Mark

Twain's "awareness that self-realization at the expense of the community's stability causes moral as well as physical isolation from it."[5] Whereas Blues, defining alienation in an absolute sense, sees Twain's early protagonists as achieving compromise without "alienation," without having to turn their backs on the community, this study, defining alienation in a relative sense, sees Twain's narrative personae as becoming morally estranged from their communities even while remaining psychologically dependent on them, that is, as leading double lives. Participating in the community—at times even participating in acts they privately condemn—Twain's personae nevertheless refuse to admit spiritual complicity in the community's transgressions. Because they cannot automatically accept particular prevailing premises, Mark Twain's alienated characters are always conscious of their differences from others; they rarely, however, reject the world outright. Rather, their estrangement is manifested in a private loneliness: the alien's critical consciousness erects a psychological barrier between the self and others.

In Mark Twain's work such alienation is most often evinced by his first-person narrators and arises in response to the prevailing moral code. While these narrators may live, work, play, laugh, cry, and generally sympathize with their neighbors, some part of them always stands aside, critically evaluating, and either explicitly or implicitly rejecting, the way people around them treat each other. If these narrators have any characteristic in common it is their hypersensitivity to suffering; nothing causes them more anguish than to witness men's brutality to each other or to other creatures. And witnesses they almost all are. In fact, the narrators with whom I am concerned all exhibit a narrative stance the ancient rhetoricians called *martyria;* they confirm whatever they are reporting by their own experience. In doing so they reveal the depth of their emotional involvement and the anguish the sight of suffering causes them. They are lonely because, unlike the others, they cannot harden themselves to the inevitability of human pain.

---

5. Thomas Blues, *Mark Twain and the Community,* p. 1. It should be clear already that Blues and I do not agree about Twain's way of resolving his

Throughout this study I have tried to be true to Mark Twain's sensibility and to seriously consider the ideas he seriously considered—a task too often slighted by scholars who, for instance, dismiss his interest in extrasensory perception and his obsession with determinism as the neurotic flounderings of an untutored mind. I found both of importance because as I examined Twain's preferred images,[6] I discovered that he was above all concerned with *time;* he suspected that there exists more than one temporal universe and more than one self to inhabit them. He saw his experiences of extrasensory perception as indications that at least one aspect of his mind could escape his body and collapse space and time, thus freeing him from the determinist, or cause-and-effect, universe, the temporal world in which we exist and "pass" our days.

This study traces the development of Twain's conjectures, examining the alienation displayed by his first-person narrative personae and the images of spiritual respite through which they resolve it. To this end I have worked both diachronically and synchronically, for although Twain's theories developed gradually, as he tried to confront his psychological problem from a "philosophical" perspective, his preferred images anticipate his philosophical writings. Long before he described the dream-self's life in *"general space—that sea of ether which has no shores, and . . . through which you may rush forever at thought-speed"* ("No. 44, MS," p. 377, Twain's emphasis; 1905), he was celebrating escape from the restrictions of gravity and temporality in a passage describing the "luxurious rest and indolence" he experienced drifting in an open boat on Lake Tahoe, where "so empty and airy did all spaces seem

---

protagonists' conflicts with their societies. Our evaluation of the characters' problems is similar, however.

6. Both the term *preferred image* and the term *center of consciousness* are used by Gaston Bachelard in *The Poetics of Reverie: Childhood, Language, and the Cosmos* and *The Poetics of Space* to describe the way poetic metaphors reveal the intentions of the author. Claiming that for the writer "the metaphor is . . . an origin, the origin of an image which acts directly, immediately" *(Poetic Reverie,* p. 70), Bachelard argues that "a poetic image bears witness to a soul which is discovering its world, the world where it would like to live and where it deserves to live" *(Poetic Reverie,* p. 15).

below us, and so strong was the sense of floating high aloft in mid-nothingness, that we called these boat excursions 'balloon-voyages' " (*RI*, p. 544; 1872).

Water and space, which I discuss in Chapter 5, are the two most closely linked of Twain's preferred images; although his early association of still water with "airy spaces" gave way to an association of outer space with infinity, both suggest that the notion of escape from gravity bore with it a sense of ecstasy. Moreover, I find evidence throughout Twain's writings that he envisioned his own mind in spatial terms, as an important link between, on the one hand, his equation of atemporality and spiritual respite and, on the other, his theory that he has a dreaming self, a far more creative self than his waking one, which can "detach itself and go wandering off upon affairs of its own."[7] In addition, Twain not only makes thematic associations between escape from concrete time and moments on water and in space,[8] he also makes rhetorical associations, manipulating tenses so that grammatical distinctions between past, present, and future are obliterated. Anticipating 44's contention in "No. 44, The Mysterious Stranger" that for the gods "there are really no divisions of time" and that the world is "built out of *thought*" ("No. 44, MS," p. 332, Twain's emphasis), Twain's images of water and space define spiritual freedom as the power both to exist beyond the material, temporal world and to effect changes in the temporal world when desired.

Grammatical detemporalization also occurs in Twain's descriptions of childhood, which I examine in Chapter 6, especially those recorded by a first-person narrator, whether he is, like Huck, a naif whose narrative method is essentially stream-of-consciousness or, like Twain in his *Autobiography*, a sophisticated remembrancer of things past. In *Adventures of Huckleberry Finn*, for instance, the freedom of Huck's vernacular speech patterns allows Twain to scramble grammatical sequences so that distinctions between time periods and between

7. Unpublished notebook, notebook number 32I, p. 3. Mark Twain Papers, Bancroft Library, University of California, Berkeley.

8. Unlike most critics of Mark Twain, I have not restricted my analysis of his water imagery to rivers. Mark Twain "valorized" (a Bachelardian word connoting celebration) moments on water because they took him not only "away

subject and object are obliterated, thus creating brief "moments of eternity" within concrete time. When Huck describes dawn on the river he confuses past, present, and future tenses, conveying the moment as a seamless unity in which the discomfort he feels in all other situations disappears and he rests, infinitely contented, within the circle of natural plenitude. Similarly, in Twain's *Autobiography*, in a passage of nearly sixteen thousand words, all in exact parallel structure and all in the present tense, Twain retrieves ecstatic moments of his own childhood by projecting images of the child's perceptions outward from the consciousness of a first-person speaker, creating incantatory rhythms that bring back summers he spent wandering through the woods on his uncle's farm. By treating an event long past to such rhythmic and temporal variations, Twain uses his craft to show that for him the special moments of childhood exist beyond the vicissitudes of time.

My chapter on Twain's images of good women (Chapter 7) is also concerned with time, although Twain's association of these figures with atemporality is conveyed less by rhetorical than by thematic means. Just as images of water, space, and childhood offer psychological respite, so too do Twain's images of good women. Like other Victorian writers, Twain sees good women as representing timeless qualities of love and care, and it should quickly become evident that this chapter only concerns Twain's "good" women because only they operate as symbols of sanity and redemption for their men. Because it focuses on the conventionally good woman, however, this chapter ignores many other female figures in Twain's work, the most obvious omission being Roxana, from *Pudd'nhead Wilson*. I have purposely not discussed Roxana because, being black, she is automatically excluded from the category "good woman" in Twain's mind; moreover, she functions as the focus for an attack on slavery, not as an agent of spiritual redemption for a distraught male character. One could argue that Faulkner's Dilsey represents timeless redemption both as a black and as a female, but not Twain's Roxana. She belongs with those characters Twain uses to exhibit the cruelties of an oppressive system,

---

from" (via the river's current) civilization but also "out of" (via the motionless, horizonless, ocean) the temporal universe.

not with the women who help men live despite the horror they feel at their entrapment in a remorseless temporal universe. By embodying reality for men who doubt the substantiality of any temporal universe and who consequently suspect they are going mad, Twain's good women provide what "peace and contentment" his men can find in this world.

Finally, my last chapter considers the concept of atemporality inherent in all Twain's preferred images in the context of his interest in those pseudosciences and other quasi-philosophical movements that rest on the assumption that the human mind can escape the restrictions of the flesh: his fascination with dreams, his experiments in mental telepathy, his interest in the "mind-cure," his dabbling with spiritualism and phrenology, his persistent questioning of the "reality" of waking life, and his conviction that his writing was done not by his waking self but by some other self, which "directed" him even when his conscious self was in agony. Considering Twain in relation to other late-nineteenth-century investigators into the properties of mind, I note that he shared his interest in the pseudosciences with serious thinkers such as William James, whose *Principles of Psychology* (1890) exhibits the variety of psychic phenomena even "legitimate" scientists considered material for their investigations. Moreover, while Twain probably did not read the traditional philosophers of mind, he did eagerly consume popular source books on psychology, writing, for instance, a thirteen-page letter of appreciation to Sir John Adams, whose *The Herbartian Psychology Applied to Education* (1898) presents the history of current theories in lucid, lively form. Both Twain's reading and his personal experiences provided him with evidence that some aspect of the human mind might not be subject to the tyranny of natural law.[9] Together with his preferred

9. It is important to note that throughout this study I use the term *natural law* as Mark Twain used it: as a concept explaining scientific rather than ethical or political matters and reflecting the emphasis of the nineteenth-century Positivists on description rather than on prescription. Observe, observe, mandated Bacon, until a regularity of sequence reveals itself. It is precisely this sequencing that captured Mark Twain's imagination: he used the terms *natural law* and *automatic law* interchangeably to signal the temporal process that results in enduring things; conversely, his later quest for escape from temporality sought the eternal entities antecedent to process, to temporality. Meanwhile, when he spoke of Natural Law he signaled his belief that temporality

images, grammatical detemporalizations, and narrative attitudes, Twain's interest in the properties of mind anticipates his late solipsism. Furthermore, there is evidence that in his last years Twain may have believed that he really *did* have another self that would exist, freed from the limitations of space and time, once his mortal self had disappeared.

Since Twain's preferred images are most frequently evoked by first-person narrators, providing psychic respite when the narrators are deeply disturbed by the events around them, I begin this study by examining the attitudes of four of Twain's first-person narrators to the communities in which they find themselves. The narrative persona with whom I am concerned in this study, that is, the morally involved narrator for whom images of water, space, childhood, or good women provide release from anxiety, becomes spiritually alienated from his contemporaries through the interaction of three factors: his intense personal sensitivity, which makes him judge events in terms of how much pain they inflict on him or on others; his feeling that he is socially different from everyone else, which predisposes him to perceive himself as an outcast; and his ability to read and write, an ability he must have in order to tell his story, but one that severs him spiritually from the people he writes about. Appraising the significance of human acts as part of his narrative function, he rejects the values of the people whose actions he condemns. In refusing complicity, however, he also finds that he loses the security that shared values bring to the participant in a human community. Consequently, this narrator feels that he is a spiritual exile, one who is always ill at ease among his contemporaries.

In response to the tension generated by his awareness of his

---

mandates irreversible causal chains.

    As I stress throughout this book, Twain was neither trained in philosophical thought nor careful about his distinctions. Thus, although he does not refer to the philosopher's definition of Natural Law—roughly, that the normative action for a given entity is determined by its nature—this concept does enter into his pessimistic pronouncements on the immutability of human nature. Similarly, his evaluation of the Moral Sense reflects the theologian's definition

own isolation, each narrator seeks a situation in which he can find relief from his anxieties. Morally justified, but spiritually alone, he searches for a means to ease the pain of his exile. Each narrator finds respite from his immediate crisis through an image or cluster of images that connotes tranquillity and security to him. His preferred image becomes the matrix of a poetic metaphor that expands into a reality for him, distracting him from his loneliness and permitting him to temporarily escape conflicts rooted in his rejection of contemporary values. Through his preferred images he conveys his conviction that for him spiritual respite and moral certainty can only be found in a realm untouched by the effects of concrete time; since he associates either childhood, women, water, or space with immutability, his preferred image signifies removal from the sequence of human change. Hank Morgan's discovery of familial love in *A Connecticut Yankee in King Arthur's Court,* for instance, becomes the matrix from which he creates a dream of domestic repose that denies the reality of the society in which he lives. When he transforms the Knights of the Round Table into a baseball team he transforms an actual society into an ideal one, and the community he perceives during his idyll with his wife and child is not the same as the one he perceives when he is not with them. Similarly, each of Twain's narrative personae discovers images of psychological transcendence through which he escapes the isolation demanded by his narrative responsibilities. Like the Creator who possesses free will himself even if he does not grant it to his creation, he provides himself with a "way out" of his fictional cosmos through his preferred images. The creative act, in other words, at once exacerbates and alleviates the artist's alienation.

Part I of this study is thus primarily a new critical reading of four novels in terms of narrative point of view. I have chosen to examine *Personal Recollections of Joan of Arc by The Sieur Louis de Conte,* "No. 44, The Mysterious Stranger," *A Connecticut Yankee in King Arthur's Court,* and *Adventures of Huckleberry Finn* out of chronological sequence because I believe that by looking at the less famous works first we can establish some of

---

that the operation of Natural Law in man's nature binds him to certain moral obligations.

the continuities, or typical elements, that the plethora of critical commentary on the more famous has tended to obscure. In addition we can see how Twain's preferred images function within a relatively fresh context before reexamining the limits to which they are pushed in the best known works.

Part II studies each of these images in depth, combining historical and rhetorical criticism with phenomenological consideration of the generative power of poetic figures. Although it has been used rarely—and then tentatively—in most American literary criticism,[10] Gaston Bachelard's phenomenological approach to poetic images is an immensely fruitful means of elucidating the connotations of rhetorical figures in an individual writer's work and of bringing together images composed at disparate periods of time in order to trace their development. Bachelard's approach is not, however, one that can be transformed into a methodology; perhaps its fruitfulness—as well as its danger—stems from the fact that each critic is at liberty to let it help her or him discover some of the hidden dimensions of the text under consideration without being confined to a set of critical rules. I have found Bachelard's *The Poetics of Reverie* and *The Poetics of Space* most liberating because they have helped me address Twain's images of childhood, water, and space; I have chosen not to work with *The Psychoanalysis of Fire* because I do not intend an elemental study of Mark Twain. In addition to Bachelard I have found sections of Maurice Merleau-Ponty's *Phenomenology of Perception* equally helpful, especially in my analyses of Twain's associations of water, space, and temporality. To a lesser extent, Georges Poulet's *Studies in Human Time* and Mircea Eliade's *The Myth of the Eternal Return* have also helped me clarify the themes I perceive in Twain's work.

My study remains, however, predominantly traditional in approach, concentrating on Twain's narrative strategies and significant images, and deeply indebted to the works of Henry Nash Smith, Roger B. Salomon, Hamlin Hill, and Alan Gribben, among others. I believe that by drawing on phenomenological insights we can better understand some of Mark Twain's liter-

10. A notable exception to this is H. Daniel Peck's *A World By Itself: The Pastoral Moment in Cooper's Fiction.*

ary responses to his psychological problems; however, if we do not fuse those insights to traditional rhetorical analysis, and ground that analysis in some sense of Twain's historical context, we risk missing the brilliance of this particular writer. Mark Twain's primary gift to us is his language: his figures of speech, his experiments with dialect, his narrative strategies, even his sentence structures and, at times, his punctuation. If we subordinate attention to these acts to an analysis of his "philosophical" writings all we discover is that Mark Twain was neither an original, a logical, nor even a very interesting thinker. If we examine his language experiments first, however, we see how his art simultaneously cradles his tensions and generates his resolutions. For this reason I first examine Twain's narrative strategies, showing how his narrative personae exhibit his alienation. Subsequently I examine the preferred images that generate his resolutions; only then do I bring phenomenological insights to bear on these images in an attempt to elucidate the philosophy of mind they suggest. By examining a variety of Mark Twain's writings through this methodological fusion, I believe we can trace his persistent use of specific images and determine what they meant to him.

Preface

Since the publication in 1973 of Hamlin Hill's *Mark Twain: God's Fool*, his biography of Mark Twain's last, hitherto little-known ten years, readers have been revising their image of the writer. Albert Bigelow Paine, the only biographer to have discussed Twain's last decade prior to the publication of Hill's book, had deliberately omitted much material detrimental to Twain's image; Hill, taking advantage of the materials left to the Mark Twain Papers in 1962, after the death of Twain's last surviving child, included what had been omitted by Paine.[1] Thus under Hill's brush Paine's portrait has been redrawn; we now see an explosive, paranoid old man who saw slights where they may not have existed, railed at cruelty and injustice, turned on himself in a bathos of guilt when family and friends suffered, and manifested his frustrations literarily in a series of scatological attacks on God, the universe, and the human race. While Hill's reading of the materials in the papers may overstate the case for Twain's instability, it is clear that for all the honors heaped upon him and all the social occasions he enjoyed, Twain's last decade was turbulent and unhappy.

Although Twain's misfortunes are certainly at the heart of much of his writing after 1896, the year his eldest daughter died, and while many of his unfinished manuscripts exhibit unmistakably autobiographical narrative patterns, the alienation evident in his late writings was not a development merely consequent upon old age and misfortune. Certainly the disgust and frustration with which Mark Twain monitored contemporary events became more marked in his last decade than ever before; nevertheless it is evident as early as 1870, when he attacked the widespread cruelty shown Chinese immigrants in San Francisco.[2] The progressive violence in his responses to moral issues

---

1. Justin Kaplan's *Mr. Clemens and Mark Twain: A Biography* does not devote sufficient space to Twain's last decade to have altered previous conceptions of that period.

2. For one of Twain's early attacks on the conduct of his contemporaries, see "Disgraceful Persecution of a Boy," first published in *Galaxy* magazine in 1870.

over the decades is an index to his progressive frustration about the possibility of moral reform: the relative gentleness of the early work suggests belief in the possibility of moral conversion; the vituperation of the late essays suggests that he had lost whatever faith he had. Throughout his work the suggestion that men are *innately* evil made him want to dissociate himself from the human race. While the voice that expresses his repulsion is intermittently evident among those that speak in many of the travel narratives, essays, and private papers, it is most consistently revealed by the stance of many of the first-person narrators of his long fiction. Projecting a fictional world, these narrators reflect their creator's own anxieties; like Mark Twain, they all want to broadcast the differences between themselves and everyone around them.

But narrative alienation is not merely an index to Twain's emotions. It is also a sign of his theory of creativity. For Twain, self-consciousness was a crucial factor in determining individual worth. Much of his anger stems from the fact that he expected the divided consciousness he experienced himself to be experienced by everyone else; torn by his own contradictions, the smug self-satisfaction of others enraged him. His own sensitivity to the ills of the world was so acute that while the entertainer he chose to be craved popular applause and financial rewards, the minister he thought he had rejected still felt compelled not only to speak out against but also to suffer for the generally miserable state of humanity. This latter attitude is manifested in Twain's strained awareness of the chasm between his own sensibility and the general insensitivity surrounding him, and his first-person personae reflect this side of his nature. In fact, without it they could not tell their stories. Mark Twain's first-person personae exhibit his discovery that the writer who would preach cannot also live comfortably

---

Mark Twain: Letters from the Earth (New York: Harper and Row, 1942), edited by Bernard DeVoto, contains representative samples from Twain's late, dark writings; *Mark Twain's Which Was the Dream? and Other Symbolic Writings of the Later Years*, edited by John S. Tuckey (Berkeley: University of California Press, 1968) contains an excellent selection.

among the people to whom his message is directed. In addition, they discover that their alienation is inseparable from their ability to record and judge the events they experience. On the one hand, all of their narratives demonstrate their progressive disaffection from their companions; on the other, only this disaffection gives them the distance they need to organize their material and tell a coherent tale. Alienation, then, is the key to much narrative patterning and imagery in these works: it is simultaneously caused by the situation in which the narrators find themselves, increased by the exigencies of their reportorial task, and resolved by the discovery of images that render access to spiritual or psychological transcendence. Thus these narrators solve their psychological problem artistically, projecting a new world that exists beyond their particular historical moments.

1

Joan of Arc: The Sieur Louis de Conte

Although Albert Bigelow Paine thought *Personal Recollections of Joan of Arc by The Sieur Louis de Conte* (1896) to be "Mark Twain's supreme literary expression,"[1] most readers have ranked it well down on the list of Mark Twain's work, considering it to possess little literary or historical merit. Ostensibly a fictionalized biography of Joan, it does not succeed in adequately characterizing her, largely because the first-person narrator cannot conceive of her in other than saintly terms. Seeing Joan as "unique" and "flawless," he is unable to penetrate her mystery and consequently fails to re-create the drama of her spiritual journey.

Rather than dismissing *Joan of Arc* for its lack of insight into the life of the saint, however, we should look beyond Mark Twain's intentions to his achievements, recognizing that the novel's "real" story lies not in de Conte's adulation of Joan but in his portrayal of himself. Even though his perspective on the events he recounts fluctuates between his adolescent and his adult points of view, he tightly structures the thematic development of his material, seeming to prove that Joan's saintliness was evident from her childhood, but actually showing how events conspired to make him the chronicler of her life. In the process he shifts the emphasis of his story, making himself, not Joan, the central character of the tale, and his alienation, rather than her elevation, its central theme. In fact, the story de Conte tells about Joan becomes far less important than the story he tells about the evolution of his own estrangement from the

1. He also thought it was "the loftiest, the most delicate, the most luminous example of [Twain's] work" (see Albert Bigelow Paine, *Mark Twain: A Biography,* 2:1029), and Twain himself, in 1908, wrote, "I like *Joan of Arc* best of all my books; and it *is* the best, I know it perfectly well" (Paine, *Mark Twain: A Biography,* 2:1034). Unfortunately, as Albert E. Stone, Jr., notes in *The Innocent*

society that condemned her. Most importantly, perhaps, the narrative patterning of de Conte's tale provides resolutions for the tensions created by Mark Twain's use of a Catholic narrator to communicate an essentially anti-Catholic theme. In championing Joan, Twain's hero must reject not only the faction of the Church that condemned her but also the entire historical environment Twain felt the Church had created, the zeitgeist of de Conte's world. Thus, as de Conte details the events that culminate in his becoming the narrator of Joan's history, he carefully delineates not only his literary qualifications but also his social and psychological fitness for his task. As he proceeds to justify himself, however, his narrative reveals a conceptual pattern of alienation and resolution woven from the facts of his physical life and the fantasies of his spiritual one. While seeking, first, to prove that he alone is qualified to record Joan's story and, second, to explain why Joan was executed, de Conte evolves from a naif to a cynic, learning to question, evaluate, and finally reject the values of his contemporaries. In the process, however, he also creates a means of escaping the despair to which his evaluation leads him. Collecting images from the positive moments of his childhood, he creates a mythical, spiritual landscape that stands in opposition to the historical, social landscape he denies, for like many of the protagonists in Twain's later works, he finds no possibility for moral redemption in the adult world. Ultimately he substitutes a system of values that he associates with the spiritual environment of his childhood for the system of values that he associates with the social environment of his adulthood; at the end of his story he feels he has a "home" to which he will return once the historical course of his unhappy life is finished. Hence the aged narrator can bring his story full circle, projecting his future from the details of his distant past, for having established his own position as well as the significance of his major themes and images early in his narrative, he has provided the means for spiritually transcending his historical circumstances.

In order to prove that he alone is qualified to be the historian of Joan's life, de Conte must first establish that he has enough

---

Eye: Childhood in Mark Twain's Imagination, Joan of Arc "has remained the least known and least read of all Twain's major novels."

distance from his material to communicate his tale in an organized fashion. Like all reliable narrators, he must prove that he can understand the implications of what he observes better than anyone else. De Conte accordingly begins his story by informing us that he has always been a foreigner in the village of Domremy. Armagnac nobles of the lower ranks, his family fled their home near Paris to Neufchateau when the rival Burgundians gained power. At six he was orphaned when a band of marauding Burgundians slaughtered his family; subsequently he was sent to the village of Domremy to be raised by the local priest, who "in the course of time, taught me to read and write, and he and I were the only persons in the village who possessed this learning" (*JA*, 1:21). Thus in the novel's first chapter de Conte demonstrates that he is well qualified to comment on the conflicts of his society, since he is a stranger to both parties with which he will eventually have to deal: the power structure of France, which Joan will defy, and the villagers of Domremy, none of whom shares his rank or his literacy.

Despite his unique position, de Conte is not uncomfortable in Domremy. Rather, he is an established member of the band of local children, one of Joan's early companions, a position that will later help him interpret the significance of her life. Meanwhile, he plays with the others on an almost equal and always easy basis. Although they call him "The Scholar," he realizes that "all children have nicknames"; unlike Joan, who shrinks from her labels, he does not seem embarrassed by his own. He feels so much a part of the group that he consistently refers to his years in the village as "peaceful and pleasant, those young and smoothly-flowing days of ours" (*JA*, 1:66).

In addition to proving his own qualifications for being the narrator, de Conte must establish the thematic categories within which the events of his story will fall if his narrative is to be structurally coherent. The major theme that he chooses to record from these years concerns the village children's loss of unity with the natural world through the interference of adults, here represented by the Church. At the opening of *Joan of Arc* de Conte reports that an undeclared war has long raged between Domremy children and Domremy adults over the right of the fairies who have traditionally lived in "l'Arbre Fée de Bourlemont" (the fairy tree) to maintain their residence there. The particular friends of the village children, these creatures have possessed the tree for five hundred years; the Church, however, declaring their presence a threat to Christianity, banishes them over the children's protests. De Conte presents this incident as his first significant bereavement; even though he has previously lost his family, loss of the fairies seems to affect him more profoundly. When the priest banishes the fairies, de Conte tells us that "all was lost, forever lost":

> The great tree . . . was never afterward quite as much to us as it had been before, but it was always dear; is dear to me yet when I go there now, once a year in my old age, to sit under it and bring back the lost playmates of my youth and group them about me and look upon their faces through my tears and break my heart, oh, my God! No, the place was not quite the same afterward. In one or two ways it could not be; for, the fairies' protection being gone, the spring lost much of its freshness and coldness, and more than two-thirds of its volume, and the banished serpents and stinging insects returned, and multiplied, and became a torment and have remained so to this day. (*JA*, 1:33)

Clearly one of the reasons de Conte feels the fairies' banishment more deeply than his former loss is that as long as the fairies inhabit the tree it functions as a small portion of Eden in the midst of the fallen world.[2] Although the notion of fairies points to a pagan rather than to a Christian concept of an uncorrupted landscape, the tree fuses pagan and Christian symbols. Like Eden, the land near it is free of snakes (significantly, referred to as serpents) and pestering insects; the water nearby, moreover, is plentiful and pure. Under the fairies' protection the children play in a paradisiacal sphere, living, like Adam and Eve, in perfect harmony with the natural world. That adults who had once played under the tree themselves could conspire with the

---

2. My analysis of the function of the fairy tree is indebted to Albert E. Stone, Jr., who notes, in *The Innocent Eye*, that for both Joan and de Conte, the tree "signalizes childhood, happiness, unity with nature, the past" (p. 223), that it evokes a paradise both pagan and Christian, and that it acts symbolically to redeem Joan from "time . . . old age . . . loss of faith" (p. 224). James D. Wilson's "In Quest of Redemptive Vision: Mark Twain's *Joan of Arc*" also notes that the tree is the incarnation of youth, faith, and purity, and that Joan is identified with

priest to ruin this spot gives de Conte his first evidence that maturation is synonymous with loss of integrity and self-reliance: not only have the adults forgotten their own youth, they have ceased to rely on their own intuitions as well. In trusting the Church's judgment over their own they have lost their intuitive knowledge of the difference between good and evil. Consequently, what is truly "lost" in Domremy is the symbol of the tree as a manifestation of paradise in the villagers' lives, a symbol that had unified them and given them "a mystic privilege not granted to any others of the children of this world"; that is, the privilege to receive a vision of the tree prior to their deaths that will indicate the state of their souls (*JA*, 1:26). If they are free of sin in their old age, they are blessed by "the soft picture of the Fairy Tree, clothed in a dream of golden light; and they see the bloomy mead sloping away to the river, and to their perishing nostrils is blown faint and sweet the fragrance of the flowers of home" (*JA*, 1:27). Until the fairies are banished the tree is a symbol of redemption for the whole village because it functions to bring their lives full circle: it is a sign that the unity with nature that they had known as children exists on the other side of death.

Thus in *Joan of Arc* de Conte not only establishes his narrative stance and dominant themes early in the novel, he also establishes the images through which he will communicate his alienation and, ultimately, his redemption. Here, *home,* a key word connoting security and tranquillity to Mark Twain as well as to most of his contemporaries, is carefully associated with nature, innocence, and childhood. Moreover, de Conte also associates Joan with the fairy tree, especially after he realizes that she meets with her supernatural visitors beneath its spreading branches. In her simple faith and moral courage she evokes the virtues the tree represents. After the fairies are exiled Joan's image becomes fused with de Conte's memories of the tree; her existence serves as a reminder of its moral influence in a world of increasing violence and terror.[3] The extent to which Joan

it. In addition to agreeing with these insights, I feel that the tree functions to redeem *all* its "children" who have not lost faith in its powers.

3. Both James D. Wilson and Roger B. Salomon see Joan and the tree as intimately associated. Moreover, in *Twain and the Image of History,* Roger B.

apotheosizes the tree, however, is inversely related to its power to influence the rest of the village. When the Fairies are banished, de Conte's generation becomes the last to be blessed with the vision; they carry their memories with them as they pass their lives in what de Conte regards as a state of exile. These children are the last of their spiritual line, and they never, in effect, grow up. Either they die young, like Joan, or they live to old age, like de Conte, but they never marry, never take their place within the community or in the continuity of human life.

For de Conte, loss of the fairies increases the estrangement that began with the circumstances of his birth. When he was an orphaned child the tree represented a "home" offering respite from the terrors of the Hundred Years' War; when he is an adolescent the figure of Joan offers him a similar center of consciousness. Both symbols are destroyed by the power of the Church. By the time he reaches old age de Conte believes that he has lost not only the companions of his youth, but the ability to share his contemporaries' values as well.

De Conte's sensitivity, his social class, and his literacy are crucial to his psychological dispossession because they equip him to be the only one to hear, see, understand, and record the complexities of Joan's career, thus making him feel that he alone understands the real moral issues of the age. As the Maid's friend, lieutenant, and scribe, he transmits her orders; without him she might not have been able to begin her famous journey toward martyrdom. His peculiar sensitivity to her is first manifested when she begins prophesying in her early adolescence. The first prophecy, according to him, occurs while the children are planning when they will go off to war. One of the boys predicts that Joan's brother will go in five years. Joan, de Conte remembers, in a "low voice and musingly," remarks, "he will go sooner." A few minutes later she makes a second murmured

---

Salomon also treats Joan as a protagonist whose importance to Twain was that she existed "outside the web of historical causality" (p. 174). In addition, Salomon notes that in this novel Twain uses de Conte as a means *not* to address the historical problem; according to him de Conte's voice, alternating between a medieval and a modern point of view, presents irreconcilably opposite views of miraculous occurrences (pp. 180–82). My study of Twain's images of respite is greatly indebted to Salomon's work; his study was the original impetus behind

presage of the future, speaking "as one who talks to himself aloud without knowing it, and none heard it but me." The third and fourth times, too, he is the only one close enough to hear her low tones. Meanwhile, his nobility is noted when one of the boys suggests that he go to war because "We've got *one* gentleman in the commune, at any rate . . . he can be an officer" (*JA*, 1:74–75, Twain's emphasis).

This brief passage introduces all the themes that will mark the relationship between Joan and de Conte throughout her life. Time and again he is the "only one" to hear or understand Joan's words; in addition to being the only one to hear her first murmured prophecies, he is the only one to see the "white shadow" of the Archangel Michael when that divine being visits Joan under the tree; the only one, years later, to understand Joan immediately when she predicts her own death, and the only one ever to realize that he must accept it. The others, he claims, wanted to forget that she had foretold her death, "and all had succeeded . . . all but me alone. I must carry my awful secret without any to help me. A heavy load, a bitter burden; and would cost me a daily heart-break" (*JA*, 2:5).

De Conte's rank and literacy become important for the evolution of his role when Joan's voices command her to leave the village and head the armies of France. According to de Conte, he is the only villager who can aid her; she "chooses" him to help her gain access to the governor of the neighboring town. Joan asks de Conte to precede her to Vaucouleurs, "for if the governor will not receive me I will dictate a letter to him, and so must have some one by me who knows the art of how to write and spell the words" (*JA*, 1:95). Furthermore, although her modesty forbids her to ask de Conte to directly introduce her to the governor, de Conte reminds us that "she knew that the governor, being a noble, would grant me, another noble, audience"—which indeed he does, although Joan does not ask de Conte to intercede for her then. Meanwhile, the peasant girl and the nobleman have privately exchanged positions: "Like the other villagers," de Conte remarks, "she had always accorded

my investigation into image clusters that represent Twain's imaginative escape from the historical problems that Salomon elucidates.

me the deference due my rank; but now, without word said on either side, she and I changed places; she gave orders, not suggestions. I received them with the deference due a superior, and obeyed them without comment" (*JA*, 1:95).

Thus de Conte's sensitivity, literacy, and rank serve to make him more useful to Joan than anyone else; they also, however, serve to isolate him from his peers. The role reversal that begins before Joan and de Conte leave Domremy continues throughout Joan's life; moreover, in order to stay near her de Conte is compelled to sever all his ties to the nobility who oppose her. Eventually, the friends of their childhood die or disappear, and de Conte, disguised as a secretary for the chief recorder at Joan's trial, finds himself the only one of all the original crowd from Domremy left to observe it. "It was a strange position for me—clerk to the recorder," he notes, "and dangerous if my sympathies and late employment should be found out. But there was not much danger. Manchon [his employer] was at bottom friendly to Joan and would not betray me; and my name would not, for I had discarded my surname and retained only my given one, like a person of low degree" (*JA*, 2:115). But having discarded the vestiges of his social position (his surname), after Joan's execution de Conte, orphaned, friendless, and bereft of his nobility, also finds that he is the "only" true believer left in a spiritually corrupt world. Sitting in the courtroom, disguised as a member of the opposition, he had been forced to rely on his own assessments of the arguments during Joan's trial. Unlike the adults of Domremy, he does not forget the spiritual lessons he learned as a child beneath the fairy tree; like Joan, he adheres to his own intuitions of truth instead of letting himself be convinced by the arguments of the priests. His disgust at the prosecutor's casuistries eventually undermines his faith in the Church, and though he lives to fight for France and to take part in Joan's Rehabilitation—her vindication, the official clearing of the charges against her—he does so for her sake, not for the Church or his country. Finally, a social and spiritual isolate, his only recourse is cynicism about the confusion of moral and political issues that led to Joan's death. Disaffected from the values of his contemporaries, he recognizes that his only function in this world is to record the tragedy of a saint persecuted by the forces of evil within her own society.

It would be a mistake to see de Conte's cynicism merely as a reflection of Twain's Protestant bias against the Catholic Church. As Albert E. Stone, Jr., notes, Twain's story is in part "a devotional exercise for a Roman Catholic girl couched in profoundly Protestant terms"[4]; the contradiction implicit in this stance reflects a major problem for any modern rationalist attempting to write from the point of view of a medieval character. Most of Twain's characters who live in the Middle Ages and therefore are Catholics reflect the contradictions between his conception of historical realism and his vision of the Church as the archvillain of Western civilization.[5] As he admits in *The Innocents Abroad*, he had been "educated to enmity toward everything that is Catholic" (*IA*, 435); reared in the prejudices of his midwest Calvinist environment, he never lost his anti-Catholicism. It was extremely difficult for him to create a sympathetic narrator who was also a faithful Catholic; often his efforts to convey a faith accepted a priori by an innocent narrator result in the character appearing to be more than a little stupid whenever the subject of the Church's teachings arises. Conse-

---

4. Stone, *The Innocent Eye*, p. 218.

5. As Salomon notes, part of Twain's problem here lies with the nineteenth-century historical sources he read in preparation for writing *Joan*, many of whom saw Joan through the Armagnac tradition that idolized and sentimentalized her. In addition, Salomon claims that neither Twain nor Michelet, the historian on whom Twain relied most heavily, was capable of understanding the spirit of the Middle Ages by reliving it sympathetically in his own mind. The problem with bringing such historical criteria—here, in particular, R. G. Collingwood's criteria for judging the value of historical periods through imaginatively re-creating them on the basis of given evidence—to bear on the work of a writer like Mark Twain is that in noting what Twain could *not* do, we ignore what he was trying to do.

The evidence of Twain's historical writings shows that his concern was for what we can loosely term "emotional history"; certainly his historical novels demonstrate far less concern for historical precision (though he was concerned to keep the "facts" as straight as possible) than for the way individuals responded to historical crises. As Collingwood notes, many current evaluations of historical periods tell us more about the historians than about the facts they evaluate (*The Idea of History* [London: Oxford University Press, 1956], p. 327). Twain's historical studies tell us that he empathized with situations that to him suggested loss, disorientation, and the attempt to find a center of consciousness to replace the one destroyed by social disruption, but that he did not empathize with figures who manifested devout faith in any system of belief. While I in no way defend Twain's pretensions to historical accuracy, I do think it is necessary to view them in the light of his intentions. Otherwise, our own imaginative

quently, de Conte's loss of faith in the visible Church is the logical resolution of the conflict between Twain's sympathies for his narrator and his own prejudices, his way of redeeming de Conte from the fallacy of false belief. Roger B. Salomon notes that as an innocent sacrificed by the practitioners of the reigning creed, Joan is presented as a type of the Christ, and Jesus' story informs Twain's narrative.[6] However, while Joan may be a type of the Christ, de Conte's unique position redeems the book from mere hagiography. The narrative logic of *Joan of Arc* supports de Conte's lapse as much as do any extrinsic factors.

Every significant action occurring late in *Joan of Arc* is anticipated earlier in the novel. First, the fairies' banishment by the Church prefigures Joan's execution by the same agency. While the tree represents a pre-Christian supernatural, and Joan, in contrast, is a soldier of Christ, the Archangel Michael's presence under the tree serves to pull both pagan and Christian mysteries together. Twain saw true Christianity as assimilating and sanctifying European nature religions, as being a heretical undercurrent in the ideology of those who oppose the power structure of the Church. Second, de Conte's spiritual loneliness after Joan's execution is anticipated both by his orphaning and by his personal response to the fairies' exile; his loss of ties to the community provides an avenue for Twain to demonstrate his narrator's progressive disaffection from all the authority figures existing in the historical world. As the lone survivor de Conte is a romantic hero who knows that God is manifested through nature rather than through doctrine and who clings to his intuitions of truth against the world's judgment.

Finally, de Conte's ability to read and write, which singles him out from the village children and makes him indispensable to Joan, also anticipates his importance as the agent of her immortality. He reveals his true mission almost defiantly: "I alone am left of those who fought at the side of Joan of Arc in the great wars. She said that I would live until these wars were forgotten—a prophecy which failed. If I should live a thousand years it would still fail. For whatsoever had touch with Joan of

---

reconstruction of his "escape from history" will be no more credible than his reconstruction of young de Conte's Catholicism.

6. Salomon, *Twain and the Image of History*, p. 178.

Arc, that thing is immortal" (*JA*, 2:284–85). It is difficult to tell if de Conte is being modest here or if he truly does not understand the import of what he is saying. Joan's prophecies have never failed before, and it is unlikely that they would fail now. Certainly de Conte, nobleman and scribe, had touch with Joan of Arc, and, like Job's messengers, he survived to tell the tale. By recording Joan's story he preserves it for later generations; moreover, he immortalizes himself in the process of immortalizing her, for his narrative proves that without him she might never have begun her journey, without him she might never have been rehabilitated, and without him she certainly would never have been given new life through the written word.

There are compensations, then, for losing one's place in one's time; immortality may be a fair exchange for the pain of learning to see through the hypocrisies of one's own historical epoch. De Conte's special burden is also his special blessing: while his unusual sensitivity to others, especially to Joan, his social rank, and above all his literacy combine to destroy his ability to accept the peculiar situation in which he finds himself, making him feel that he is an alien among his own people, the same traits also save him, for by preserving Joan's name, by identifying her with the same quality of divinity that marked the fairy tree, and, finally, by keeping the images of both before his readers as he tells a tale of historical tragedy, de Conte saves himself by preserving the idea of true paradise for an otherwise corrupt world. At the end of his narrative he tells us that he has seen the tree, and is content; he knows he will play once more in the divine landscape.

De Conte's story suggests that the historian of contemporary events, whose business it is to record and interpret the corruption of his own era, inevitably becomes isolated from his peers and must protect himself emotionally by adopting a psychologically defensive attitude. For de Conte, as for many, cynicism in part serves this function. His loneliness lacks the despair exhibited by most classic cynics, however, for by imaginatively re-creating the tree and the countryside around it as symbols standing outside the course of human history, and by immortalizing Joan as a figure inhabiting the country of grace, de Conte creates an ideal landscape that he substitutes for the actual one

2

"No. 44, The Mysterious Stranger": August Feldner

Whereas in *Joan of Arc* the narrator's alienation results from his becoming the historian of someone else's life, in "No. 44, The Mysterious Stranger," August Feldner's despair results from his comprehending the responsibility he bears for his own. In 1892, when Mark Twain finished *Joan of Arc*, he could still project a complex image of salvation despite his narrator's recognition that he lived in an almost irreparably corrupt world; however, in 1908, when he abandoned the "Mysterious Stranger" manuscripts, Twain seems to have been unable to sustain any faith in the possibility of spiritual sanctuary.[1] For more than a decade after the sudden death of his oldest daughter, and in the first three years after the death of his wife, Twain's only

1. Throughout this book, unless otherwise noted, all quotations from *The Mysterious Stranger* will refer to Version D, "No. 44, The Mysterious Stranger," sometimes known as the "Print Shop" version, and not to the version edited —and bowdlerized—by Albert Bigelow Paine and Frederick Duneka in 1916. "No. 44, The Mysterious Stranger," with two other manuscript versions as well as the editorial history of the text, can be found in William M. Gibson's edition of *Mark Twain: The Mysterious Stranger* (Berkeley: The University of California Press, 1969). Like most of Twain's work, this manuscript was composed in bits and chunks, between 1902 and 1908. The Gibson edition places the chapter Twain wrote in 1904 and labeled "Conclusion of the book" after the historical parade of skeletons, written in 1908. The version generally referred to, the Paine/Duneka version, is a compound of an earlier manuscript that Gibson titles "The Chronicle of Young Satan" and the last "solipsistic" chapter that Gibson has determined was intended for the "Print Shop" version.

Although the Gibson edition has now been available for over ten years, and although John S. Tuckey's *Mark Twain and Little Satan: The Writing of The Mysterious Stranger* was published in 1963, most critics have continued to refer to the Paine/Duneka version. Recently, however, Sholom Kahn, in *Mark Twain's Mysterious Stranger: A Study of the Manuscript Texts*, has given us a detailed analysis of all the manuscripts, and it is to be hoped that his study will stimulate the urgently needed reconsideration of them. William R. Macnaughton's *Mark Twain's Last Years as a Writer* has begun this reversal by

hope for peace seemed to lie in an image of freedom from the human condition; in "No. 44, The Mysterious Stranger," however, even that freedom seems as much a curse as a blessing. "No. 44, The Mysterious Stranger" is Twain's most complex unfinished novel; yet his narrator's education, and his image of escape, constitutes one of Twain's most vivid representations of his own spiritual quest.

As a small boy in Eseldorf (Assville, to us), a village that "drowsed in peace in the deep privacy of a hilly and woodsy solitude where news from the world hardly ever came to disturb its dreams, and was infinitely content" ("No. 44, MS," p. 221), August Feldner, the narrator of "No. 44, The Mysterious Stranger," claims that, like the other boys, he once had been "in paradise." At the time the story opens, however, he is removed from that serenity because he is learning a trade that he describes as making him feel "more curiously than pleasantly situated" ("No. 44, MS," p. 229).

The trade is printing, and August, like de Conte, is distinguished from his early peasant playmates by the fact that he can read and write. August never mentions his parents or any ascribed rank he may possess, but because he is an apprentice printer in the time of medieval guilds, he has assumed a professional rank. In his care to establish just *how* select his profession is, he also establishes the fact that it is a potentially dangerous one. Printing, he tells us,

> was a new art [the year is 1490], being only thirty or forty years old, and almost unknown in Austria. Very few persons in our secluded region had even seen a printed page, few had any clear idea about the art of printing, and perhaps still fewer had any curiosity concerning it or felt any interest in it. Yet we had to conduct our business with some degree of privacy, on account of the Church. The Church was opposed to the cheapening of books and the indiscriminate dissemination of knowledge. ("No. 44, MS," pp. 229–30)

As this passage illustrates, August and his fellow printers are conspicuous within the village because, unlike the other "asses," they know "an abstruse science." In *Joan of Arc*, de Conte's literacy earned him respect among the villagers. His

---

relying on Tuckey, Gibson, and Kahn when his study refers to *The Mysterious Stranger*.

position, though special, was not antagonistic, and his loneliness did not evolve until his friends disappeared. In "No. 44, The Mysterious Stranger," however, literacy is potentially dangerous to its possessors. Though the villagers may not care what the printers are publishing, the Church does, and from the printers' point of view the villagers are dangerous because —being asses—they are unable to think for themselves; consequently the priests could easily whip them into a holy war against literacy. The printers' esoteric knowledge, rather than making them literati, makes them objects of suspicion, and they find it safest to leave the village altogether, eventually making their home in an abandoned castle situated on a precipice overlooking the river: "prodigious, vine-clad, stately and beautiful, but mouldering to ruin" ("No. 44, MS," p. 229). In "No. 44, The Mysterious Stranger," the printer's art removes its practitioners from the community and puts them, literally, on a precipice overlooking the common world.[2]

For August, then, being professionally associated with the dissemination of knowledge is dangerous. The fact that the profession is also highly selective is emphasized when his fellow printers protest their master's invitation to the stranger—who arrives disguised as a beggar—to become an apprentice. When the master "rose and solemnly laid his hand upon the lad's shoulder like a king delivering the accolade," August records, "every man jumped to his feet excited and affronted, to protest against this outrage, this admission of a pauper and tramp without name or family to the gate leading to the proud privileges and distinctions and immunities of their great order" ("No. 44, MS," p. 252). By admitting the stranger, the printers consider that the master had "struck at their order, the apple of their eye, their pride, the darling of their hearts, their dearest possession, their nobility—as they ranked and regarded it—and degraded it" ("No. 44, MS," p. 253). The printers, in effect, use the guild to set themselves apart from the common folk. The indices to alienation here are consequently somewhat complex; the Church may hold the printers in suspicion, but they, in a

2. Sholom Kahn, too, notes that in "No. 44, MS" the village setting rapidly loses its importance for the story and that the castle is "a microcosm in which

combination of necessity and choice, in turn hold themselves aloof from everyone else.

Even within this select society August sees himself as the odd man. When he lists the printer's "family" he lists himself last—because of his modesty; because, except for a fifteen-year-old cripple, at sixteen he is the youngest person there; because, as an apprentice, he has the least status of all the printers; but mostly, we soon realize, because he feels that he is different from everyone else because he is the sensitive character who shrinks from the other printers' inexplicable nastiness. Also, as he hastens to tell us, because he is a coward; when the other printers abuse 44 (the stranger), "privately my heart bled for the boy, and I wanted to be his friend, and longed to tell him so, but I had not the courage, for I was made as most people are made, and was afraid to follow my own instincts when they ran counter to other people's. The best of us would rather be popular than right" ("No. 44, MS," p. 244). Certainly this aspect of August's character reveals Twain laboring his thesis that men are intrinsic cowards; similar lines in this and other manuscript versions of the novel have led many readers to see its major theme as an attack on the hypocrisy of social relationships and a refutation of people's motives in seeking friends. Openly admitting his cowardice, however, also serves as a means for August to reveal that in his awareness that he shares one of the most despicable of human traits, he paradoxically feels himself to be different from everyone else. His distinction lies in his consciousness of his human failings rather than in his freedom from them.[3]

While young de Conte's peculiar sensitivity to Joan only made him unhappy when he recognized that he alone knew she was going to die, August's peculiar sensitivity makes him constantly ill at ease. He makes it clear by numerous remarks

---

the struggle between light and darkness, good and evil must be fought out" (*Mark Twain's Mysterious Stranger*, pp. 102, 106).

3. Here I differ with Kahn, who feels that August's "weakness" is "an excessive concern with reputation." I think August's problem must be seen in its larger context as one of the means by which Twain demarcates the sensitive individual in an evil society. In addition, Kahn is at some pains to develop a theme that he sees as exploring master/servant relationships and, on a deeper level, black/white ones. While there are references—most of them deliberately anachronistic—to blacks in "No. 44, MS" (especially 44's minstrel show), I do not see this as a theme.

indicating his disapproval of the printers' behavior that even though he is with them he is never of them. Despite his disapproval, however, he reveals his uneasiness about his companions indirectly, generally by describing their behavior rather than by openly condemning them; his rhetorical subterfuge is a sign of his insecurity about his relationship to them. While he does tell us that most of them are "surly," "quarrelsome," "malicious," "hateful," and prone to drunkenness, and that the master, an essentially kindly man, is ruled by his second wife, a "masterly devil," often he implies the state of conflict in the castle by more subtle means. Always ironic in his use of the word *family*, for instance, he slips suggestions about the nature of this one into all his descriptions of their environment; the great room with the spectacular view "we used as dining room, drinking room, quarreling room—in a word, family room," he tells us. "With a cart-load of logs blazing here within and a snow-tempest howling and whirling outside, it was a heaven of a place for comfort and contentment and cosiness, and the exchange of injurious personalities" ("No. 44, MS," p. 234). August's rhetorical subterfuge also supports his image of himself as an impotent coward. When he notes how often and how cruelly the printers haze 44 and how little he can do to prevent it, he reminds us that "I should have been despised if I had befriended him; and I should have been treated as he was, too" ("No. 44, MS," p. 245). His sympathy for the outcast suggests how deeply he feels like one himself.

The crucial difference between August's and 44's conflicts with the other characters, however, anticipates Twain's solipsistic resolution to August's cosmic problem in the final chapters of the book. While 44 is *really* being set upon by the printers, August's difficulties are almost all imaginary. Rarely do the others attack him as they do 44, and then only when they suspect him of duplicity. In fact, it is hard to determine exactly how much they do antagonize him, because he seems to overreact to the slightest provocation. For instance, when the other printers call him by "an unprintable name . . . it stung me and embittered me more than any of the other hurts and humiliations that were put upon me; and I was girl-boy enough to cry about it, which delighted the men beyond belief, and they rubbed their hands and shrieked with delight" ("No. 44, MS," p. 263).[4] A receptiveness to injury like this points to intense subjectivity, precisely the narrative point of view Twain needs to prepare the grounds for his conclusion. If August initially perceives only those aspects of the world that pertain to him, distorting even those into a paranoid vision, the author should have little difficulty in pointing out that everything else August thinks he perceives exists only in his mind also.

Because he is so intensely sensitive himself, August has difficulty understanding 44's serenity, for the stranger, being immune to social criticism, does not share his terrors. After the men have declared a strike in retaliation for the master's kindness to the stranger, August notes that "wherever 44 came he got ugly looks, threatening looks, and I was afraid for him and wanted to show sympathy but was too timid. I tried to think I avoided him for his own good, but did not succeed to my satisfaction. As usual, he did not seem to know he was being so scowled at and hated" ("No. 44, MS," p.288). For August, perhaps one of the first proofs of 44's otherworldliness is his indifference to being ostracized. "As the days went along, everybody talked about 44, everybody observed him, everybody puzzled over him and his ways; but it was not discoverable that he ever concerned himself in the least degree about this or was in any way interested in what people thought of him or said about him. This indifference irritated the herd, but the boy did not seem aware of it" ("No. 44, MS," p. 244). Although August claims to want to be like 44 in order to be envied, for "to be envied is the secret longing of pretty much all human beings," one suspects that he would like 44's callousness to human cruelty even more. The major talent 44 possesses that August covets is the inability to feel.

August's position is similar to de Conte's in that both narrators stand out within a group that is itself in opposition to those having real power in their society. In both cases class and literacy serve to distinguish them from their early peasant comrades,

---

4. According to Gibson's introduction to the manuscripts, Twain marginally noted "Bottle-a'd" by this passage; the full printer's term is "bottle-assed." Gibson also thinks that August speaks for Twain here. While it *is* a derogatory

and in both cases the differences are emphasized by their personal sensitivity to the figure who, being more than human, provides the book's focus. In both cases the combination of sensitivity and literacy creates the character who can record the fantastic incidents that occur, that is, those qualifications are what make the narrator the only character who can write the book. And in both cases this character is the only one who, like Melville's Ishmael, survives to tell the tale. But August exhibits a degree of agonized self-consciousness that finally makes him an even more alienated character than de Conte. His estrangement from the other people whom he essentially abhors (as de Conte initially does not) is so extreme that what little nostalgia he shows is for the brief period when he seems to have lacked any consciousness of individuality, for the edenic time before his apprenticeship when he, too, was an "ass" and played, if not in a paradise radiating from a magical tree, at least in a landscape removed from the pressures of adult life. His elevation into the literate professional ranks merely seems to have engendered a progressively painful sensitivity.

Much of de Conte's story is told from the perspective of an embittered old age, but at least he knows that his spiritual future lies in a divine landscape. In "No. 44, The Mysterious Stranger," however, the search for a landscape of salvation presents a far more serious problem for August because by the end of his story there is no material left from which he can construct an alternative to the corrupt historical world that he finally learns is an illusion. In 1892, at the time he was writing *Joan of Arc*, Twain could still entertain the possibility that good, though in battle with evil, was nevertheless inherent in human nature. Characters like de Conte were capable of recognizing it intuitively, and their existence testified to the possibility that evil might yet be conquered and good reinstituted as a first cause. If the ideal order and ideal values represented by Joan and the fairy tree could be realized on earth, all subsequent acts might spring from them and human lives might achieve their moral potential.

In "No. 44, The Mysterious Stranger," however, the stranger

term, only a hypersensitive sixteen-year-old would find it painful enough to cry about.

does not represent a new moral order. Rather, for Twain the significance of 44 lies both in his immortality and in his amorality, because both signal freedom from the human condition. Forty-four is neither subject to death nor possessed of the moral sense, a faculty that Twain sees as enabling its possessors to discriminate between good and evil only to enable them to choose evil. By the time he wrote the "Mysterious Stranger," Twain was not only a professed determinist, he also was no longer certain that any inherent human good remained to be intuited, and he saw no way out of the human dilemma short of destroying the automatic, or natural, law that he believed made the consequences of any act inevitable.[5] Since natural law takes effect in time, through cause-and-effect sequencing, Twain reasoned that only by destroying time could we confront and destroy the first cause. Consequently, much of 44's function in "No. 44, The Mysterious Stranger" is to prove to August that it is possible to annihilate temporal distinctions.

The fact that there is little continuity to the sequence of events narrated in "No. 44, The Mysterious Stranger" is a reflection of Twain's concern with the abolition of time and as part of the book's theme complements both August's intense subjectivity and his loss of faith in contemporary values.[6] Not only can 44 move back and forth between historical epochs —one morning, for instance, he appears in August's room with a breakfast of hot corn pone and fried spring chicken—but he also has the power to put August to sleep for periods that, though extremely brief, thoroughly rejuvenate him. After one "nap," August tells us,

5. In *Mark Twain's Last Years as a Writer*, Macnaughton tries very hard to prove that in his last years Twain was not a completely convinced pessimist; though I admire Macnaughton's scholarship, I cannot agree with most of his conclusions. Certainly Twain (as he always had done) abandoned many of his manuscripts because of extrinsic, rather than intrinsic factors. Nevertheless, the manuscripts, the finished works, and the notebooks of those years all, it seems to me, point to a profound loss of faith in human potential.

6. Kahn, too, senses that Twain was concerned with the problem of time in this novel, but he does not pursue the theme consistently. Rather, after noting that "after chapter 18 the movement away from calendar time leads toward a return to the past, involving both personal memory and universal history" (*Mark Twain's Mysterious Stranger*, p. 150), he discusses chapters 23–27, which concern a bizarre courtship entanglement. Kahn does, later, note that in the procession 44's perception of time is significantly different from normal (p. 177).

I woke up fresh and fine and vigorous, and found I had been asleep little more than six minutes. The sleeps which he furnished had no dependence upon time, no connection with it, no relation to it; sometimes they did their work in one interval, sometimes in another, sometimes in half a second, sometimes in half a day . . . but let the interval be long or short, the result was the same, that is to say, the reinvigoration was perfect, the physical and mental refreshment complete. ("No. 44, MS," p. 363)

Through 44, August learns that linear time can be circumvented, and the story he narrates, like the naps 44 provides, often has no dependence upon time. We do not know if the events in the castle occur over a month or a year; since there is almost no connection between them and the external world, relative time spans seem irrelevant. In another version of "The Mysterious Stranger," "The Chronicle of Young Satan" (much of which figures into the Paine/Duneka version), Philip Traum (44) educates Theodor (August) by taking him on trips to see the appalling consequences of the human moral sense, erasing the amount of linear time that the journeys take. "He flashed me around the globe," Theodor recalls, "stopping an hour or a week, at intervals, in one or another strange country, and doing the whole journey in a few minutes by the clock" ("CYS," p. 167). The narrator's education is thus ultimately not, as early readers perceived, limited to a recognition of the absurdity of the human moral sense; rather, it leads him to the perception that true spiritual freedom from the human condition lies in liberation from the restrictions of chronology.[7]

7. See Roger B. Salomon, *Twain and the Image of History*, p. 207. The critical history of *The Mysterious Stranger* is complicated by the editorial history of the text. Nearly all critics, even after publication of the Gibson editions in 1969, have relied on the Paine/Duneka version, and while everyone agrees that Satan (44) is a spokesman for Twain's rejection of the moral sense, controversy has concentrated on the possibility that the concluding chapters hold forth some hope for redemption. Examples of the argument are Bernard DeVoto's now famous claim that in asserting that life was all a dream, Twain "saved himself in the end, and came back from the edge of insanity" ("The Symbols of Despair," in *Mark Twain at Work*, pp. 105–30); Ruth Miller's conclusion that at the end "Theodor [August] has a new grail—laughter" ("But Laugh or Die: A Comparison of *The Mysterious Stranger* and *Billy Budd*," p. 26); and Stanley Brodwin's assertion that *The Mysterious Stranger* expresses "the truth of man's existential confrontation of a reality he can make little sense of and that always throws himself back on himself to find truth" ("Mark Twain's Masks of Satan: The

The problem thus posed for August is that once he has decided to be 44's friend (even though he never makes the decision public) and come to share 44's cosmic secrets, he has no place to go after 44 convinces him that not only the heaven in which he believes but also the entire historical world are "made of thought." Unlike de Conte, August has no intimation that he is recording history; rather, he believes he is recording the story of his private journey to enlightenment. His theme, however, is advanced with decreasing continuity or coherence of plot. Although the conflict with the Church stands behind the printers' secrecy about their craft, once August gives us that information he admits no other social or historical factors into his tale. Removed from the events of its epoch, the castle stands in a limbo on its bluff above human time, and August records the events that happen there in an almost arbitrary order. His increasingly nonlinear narrative provides one of the links between the theme of his story and the solipsism of its final chapter.

Final Phase," p. 333). Of the studies based on the Paine/Duneka versions, perhaps the closest to my position is Edwin Fussell's "The Structural Problem of *The Mysterious Stranger*." Assuming that Twain knew how he planned to conclude the book, and therefore wrote with the final chapter always in mind, Fussell holds that "in order to render his solipsism in narrative form, Twain fell back on the time-honored dream-vision structure" (p. 77) and that Twain's "failure satisfactorily to arbitrate the claims of objective and subjective phenomena ultimately explains the basic confusion in *The Mysterious Stranger*" (p. 78). Fussell sees the theme of the story as the revelation of the unreality of reality to the narrator, and what unity the book has, as a reflection of its thematic concern with "progressive phases from unreality (literal materiality) to reality (solipsistic ideality)."

In 1963 John S. Tuckey published *Mark Twain and Little Satan: The Writing of The Mysterious Stranger*, which first pointed out that the final "solipsistic" chapter was intended for the "Print Shop" rather than the "Eseldorf" version even though it was written four years before the "Print Shop" version was completed. In the course of tracing the composition of the texts Tuckey notes that the August who learns about his immortality in the last chapter is not the boy's waking self but his dream self, and thus already freed from the strictures of time and space.

Sholom Kahn, however, suggests that the novel is ultimately about the problem of freedom: that 44 is an angel, and that his function is to educate August in the possibility that he *can* remake the human condition through what Twain called "enlightened selfishness"—activities aimed at satisfying both the subject and the community *(Mark Twain's Mysterious Stranger*, p. 187). Kahn places himself within the DeVoto tradition of *Mysterious Stranger* criticism here, and I cannot agree with his conclusions.

Yet, like de Conte, August does have a brief intuition of an alternative life; an intuition born of his education in the destructibility of concrete time. August's dream-self, a spiritual doppelgänger 44 has embodied to cover August's absences, finally confronts and begs him to "be merciful, and set me free!" The dream-self's plea to be released from this "odious flesh" achieves its poignancy not from its association of the flesh with sin but from its association of the flesh with decay; the possibility of release presented in this passage provides August with his one brief vision of escape from his dilemma. The doppelgänger refers to its embodiment as "this decaying vile matter . . . this loathsome sack of corruption . . . this rotting flesh," telling August that unembodied he is a "spirit of the air, habitant of the august Empire of Dreams," where "we do not know time, we do not know space—we live, and love, and labor, and enjoy, fifty years in an hour, while you are sleeping, snoring, repairing your crazy tissues" ("No. 44, MS," pp. 369–70). Our bodies are our surest record of the passage of time; in the Judeo-Christian world they have traditionally been seen as the prison of the spirit. Being released from the flesh is an avenue to timelessness because it is a release from the sequence of decay. Without the effects of time, their cause must also disappear, and the dream-self's ideal existence seems to present August with a joyous alternative to human history, an ideal image of a consciousness free to roam the universe without regard to time, space, the corruption of human values, or the corruption of the mortal frame.

Although the lyrical intensity of the dream-self's vision of escape from history reveals Twain's emotional commitment to that vision, in "No. 44, The Mysterious Stranger" it is proved to be a philosophical dead end. The thematic insistence that dream lives are as real as waking ones in the Paine/Duneka version of "The Mysterious Stranger" has led most readers to see the unreality of the commonsense universe as Twain's epistemological escape from the prison of history, and certainly Twain's long-term interest in dreams supports this view.[8] However,

8. Twain, a sleepwalker as a child and an insomniac as an adult, was interested in dreams throughout his life. The evolution of his concept of the dream-self is discussed in the concluding chapter of this study.

reading the Paine/Duneka version backward through the "levels of dreaming" that prepare for the last chapters, as Edwin Fussell does,[9] merely demonstrates how poor a grasp Twain had of philosophical logic. In "No. 44, The Mysterious Stranger," on the other hand, Twain moves to a more abstract level that provides a framework for the several philosophical avenues explored in the work. "No. 44, The Mysterious Stranger" is a more daring treatment of his themes because it tries to reach beyond dreams to the power that creates them.[10] August's education does not end with his understanding that only the flesh binds us to time and to the human condition. Having already demonstrated his own and the dream-self's ability to escape the restrictions of time, 44 teaches August that he, too, can be free. Furthermore, he teaches him that the liberated consciousness can annihilate time itself, set the universe back before the beginning, and start all over again.

As a demonstration of this, in the penultimate chapter, 44 makes time go backward. When he does so, August finds that his temporal being cannot endure it: "My brain was spinning, it was audibly whizzing, I rose reeling, and was falling lifeless to the floor, when 44 caught me" ("No. 44, MS," p. 398). The Stranger frees him from his flesh so that he can "look on and enjoy, taking no personal part in the backward flight of time or its return" ("No. 44, MS," p. 398). Removed from the restrictions of chronology, August *does* enjoy watching the destruction of his world, especially 44's crowning effect, the Procession of the Dead, which first destroys the historical sequence and then briefly reinstitutes it in order to review its effect on human

9. Fussell, "The Structural Problem of The Mysterious Stranger," p. 72. Even though Fussell is reading the Paine/Duneka text, I think his insights into the conclusion are relevant to us here.

10. I am greatly encouraged by Kahn's epilogue, where he suggests that even though Twain probably never read Descartes's *Meditations*, Cartesian echoes are to be found in "No. 44, MS." Certainly enough of Descartes's ideas had been filtered into the many historical, biographical, and psychological books Twain read for him to have been exposed to them—even if we are not willing to concede that he could have generated some version of the ideas himself. More importantly, perhaps, since Mark Twain had by 1904 watched his books (especially the early ones) become instrumental in the "retrieval of the past" that was one of the results of the local colorist movement, he might easily have felt that his books had, in part, *created* those bygone worlds.

beings.[11] August first becomes conscious of darkness and silence:

> all visible things gloomed down gradually, losing their outlines little by little, then disappeared utterly. The thickest and solidest and blackest darkness followed, and a silence which was so still it was as if the world was holding its breath. That deep stillness continued, and continued, minute after minute . . . after about ten minutes I heard a faint clicking sound coming as from a great distance. It came slowly nearer and nearer, and a little louder and a little louder, and increasing steadily in mass and volume, till all the place was filled with a dry sharp clacking and was right abreast of us and passing by! ("No. 44, MS," p. 401)

In effect 44 re-creates the void and then fills it with the eerie noise and sight of "continental masses" of human skeletons, each bearing a tag giving his or her name and the dates of his or her life. Each represents one aspect of the tragic folly of human pretensions, whether of the illusoriness of earthly pomp (some of the skeletons "fetched their crowns along, and had a rotten velvet rag or two dangling about their bones"); of the ephemeralness of earthly possessions (others "dragged the rotting ruins of their coffins after them by a string, and seemed pitifully anxious that their poor property shouldn't come to harm"); or of the hopelessness of earthly love (one was "a young mother whose little child disappeared one day and was never heard of again, and so her heart was broken, and she cried her life away") ("No. 44, MS," pp. 401–2). The vision is abstract in that each skeleton has been stripped of its historical "flesh" and made to represent an entire genre of human misery. And the genres are endless. August reports that the procession passes "for hours and hours"

11. Kahn sees the procession as providing a smooth link between the theme of freedom (which for him is the theme of the book) and the final chapters. But Kahn defines "freedom" as the freedom to change events in the past, whereas I see Twain defining it as escaping the confines of causality. Furthermore, Kahn does see the conclusion as optimistic, while I can see nothing but relentless pessimism there. I think the *really* important statement on which all critics can agree is that the conclusion is rhetorically and philosophically one of the most compelling final chapters in American literature. That fact, coupled with the conclusion's apparent ambiguity, will insure that the fight over its meaning will continue for a long time.

until 44 finally stops it by a wave of his hand and "we stood in an empty and soundless world."

After the procession August learns the full extent of the relationship between time and his narrative responsibilities. Through his association with 44 he has come to understand not only that everything he had believed about the nature of men's relationship to God is wrong but also that men cannot change as long as they live within a temporal framework that mandates causal sequencing, that is, as long as they are subject to natural law. Whatever is begun in time must continue through an unalterable sequence. The only way to reform mankind is to re-create the Creation, to construct a universe initially so perfect that each effect promotes greater good rather than greater evil. Since August now understands this relationship, he is prepared for 44's revelation that human history is "all a vision, a dream." His first response is "a gush of thankfulness"; but the subsequent disclosure that "nothing exists save empty space— and you" and that he, as "the only existent Thought," has the power to create new dreams, "appalls" him. Not only is there no heaven or hell—no afterlife, whether of salvation or of damnation—there is nothing at all, neither an earthly nor an unearthly landscape. According to 44, not even "the sun, the moon, the wilderness of stars" exist unless August dreams them, so the dream-self's vision of unearthly bliss, which August hoped to achieve in his new state, was as false as his temporal life of fleshly restrictions. When de Conte lost his intimacy with the history of his era by recording it, he still retained belief in a mythical landscape where he could find salvation and repose. According to 44, August's solution is to create "new dreams, and better." But with August's comprehension of his power to create new worlds must come the realization that because he is the sole creator he is responsible for all the misery of all the dreams he has had before. The terror of history lies in *him;* some evil in his imagination initiated the horror of those causal chains. Consequently, he is appalled because he realizes that he *cannot* create "better" dreams.

If Twain sees de Conte as the historian who becomes es-tranged from the culture he evaluates, he sees August as the novelist who is responsible for the worlds he creates. As fictions, novels are worlds in themselves, and in "No. 44, The Mysterious Stranger" Mark Twain portrays the novelist's imagination as a reflection of divine creativity. The writer can create worlds and destroy them, too. At the end of this novel we are left with the void, and the "empty and soundless void" illustrates the mind of the writer before he begins to dream. It is his confession of omnipotence, but in "No. 44, The Mysterious Stranger," omnipotence is equated with terror.

Since part of August's education has destroyed his faith in God, the epistemological "solution" to the problem of history in this work implies that there is no exit from the author's solipsistic vision. August is initially alienated from his environment because he is more sensitive than anyone else around him. Through his association with 44 he learns that time is the prerequisite for causality, and thus he learns the secret of the human condition. But the ultimate estrangement is alienation from the self, and at the end of his novel about the falsity of human values August is appalled because he realizes that *he* is the source of the evil that repels him. Since he cannot envision a situation that lacks evil, he cannot create an alternative to the history of human tragedy. Furthermore, as the "only existent Thought," 44 tells him, he is "inextinguishable, indestructible," and will shortly be "alone in shoreless space, to wander its limitless solitudes without friend or comrade forever" ("No. 44, MS," p. 404). Not only can he not reform himself, he cannot annihilate the consciousness that created the prison of human time. The dreamer cannot stop dreaming just because he knows he dreams. For the novelist, the dreamer of subjective worlds, as opposed to the historian, the chronicler of objective ones, true horror emanates from within rather than from without. By confessing his omnipotence Twain accepts the responsibility for his own imagination: an imagination that confronts and unmasks itself only to find that its curse is to eternally re-create worlds that mirror its own ineradicable evil. When the dreamself's vision of escape from human time is proved false, the author of this novel is faced with his own epistemological reality. In "No. 44, The Mysterious Stranger" the creator of fictions has no permanent recourse to a landscape outside of time.

3

A Connecticut Yankee in King Arthur's Court: Hank Morgan

In *A Connecticut Yankee in King Arthur's Court* (1889) the narrator is involuntarily transported out of the nineteenth century and into the sixth. Hank Morgan's "alienation," then, unlike de Conte's or August's, is a logical result of his circumstances and necessarily informs his narrative stance. Certainly it is *the* comic device of the novel; *A Connecticut Yankee's* raison d'être is to explore the clash between Hank's habits of body and mind and those of his antagonists. Whereas *Joan of Arc* and "No. 44, The Mysterious Stranger" were written as "serious" novels, *Yankee* was—at least initially—intended to be a comic one, and its protagonist a comic figure.[1] But for all his aggressiveness, and for all the humorous material that his

1. In recent years a critical controversy has raged about Hank Morgan, chiefly focusing on what Mark Twain intended by his character and which institutions—sixth-century feudalism or nineteenth-century industrialism—Twain was attacking. William Dean Howells thought the novel a "glorious gospel of equality" ("My Mark Twain," p. 44), and until recently twentieth-century critics have agreed, seeing the novel as embodying Twain's attack on monarchy, aristocracy, and the Church. Philip Foner, in *Mark Twain: Social Critic*, for instance, sees the theme as "democracy's superiority to kingship and despotism in general" (p. 113), and Louis Budd, in *Mark Twain: Social Philosopher* sees it as embodying Twain's "temporary shift from sympathy with employers to sympathy with labor" (p. 113). In *Mark Twain's Fable of Progress: Political and Economic Ideas in A Connecticut Yankee in King Arthur's Court*, Henry Nash Smith contends that Mark Twain was "asking himself whether the American Adam, who began as a representative of a preindustrial order, could make the transition to urban industrialism and enter upon a new phase of his existence by becoming a capitalist hero" (p. 69). According to Smith, Twain found that he could not show "how industrialism remakes men and institutions"; rather, Hank—and his creator—only destroys old patterns (p. 98). In *Mark Twain: The Fate of Humor*, James M. Cox, examining the tensions among the humorous patterns in the book, finds that Mark Twain's "major investment is in the Yankee's attitudes" (p. 206); however, Cox claims, the original burlesque criticism of sixth-century institutions is transformed to tragedy because it comes to reflect the frustrations in Twain's life during composition of the novel; comedy and satire became mere indignation when Twain "gave himself up" to hatred

predicament engenders, Hank also evinces a nervousness about being a misfit that links him to the narrators we have already examined. In his comments about his antagonistic relationship to other members of the community, and in his record of his brief, idyllic marriage, he demonstrates patterns of alienation and resolution similar to those of Louis de Conte and August Feldner.

Hank's position in the novel differs from de Conte's or August's because he is not merely its narrator but its focal character as well. While de Conte and August become disaffected from their societies through their association with a character who represents another world, Hank *is* that character. Furthermore, Hank's voice is more believable than de Conte's or August's because in creating him Mark Twain was not faced with the task of communicating a heretical vision through a devout speaker. Rather, Hank's disaffection is inherent both in his role (he is a foreigner in Camelot and it is appropriate for him to question everything he sees) and in his background (he is a New Englander, and both intellectual skepticism and moralistic criticism are natural modes for him). Consequently, he has ample justification for observing and for judging what he sees.

In addition, being regarded as an alien interloper is not an entirely new experience for Hank. He is not merely an alien in the sixth century, he is an eccentric in his own, a fighter who has

---

and rage (p. 207). Maxwell Geismar thinks the Yankee, as Twain's persona, finds himself "increasingly alienated from his own tearing, pushing, booming, materialistic society" (*Mark Twain: An American Prophet,* p. 111); Thomas Blues, on the other hand, thinks that Mark Twain "could not resolve an issue [concerning] whether the individual who is liberated by technology to exercise the inherent virtues of common-sense, self-reliance, and courage on behalf of the community will choose to use his power humanely or will corrupt himself in pursuit of selfishness" (*Mark Twain and the Community,* p. 39). In *Mark Twain and John Bull: The British Connection,* Howard Baetzhold, claiming that "Twain's ultimate intention will probably remain a matter of critical controversy," finds that his pessimism overtakes his reformism, and notes that "It was not so much that he had lost faith in . . . technological progress, but that he had become at least partly convinced that . . . superstition, ignorance, subservience to custom— could not be . . . rooted out" (p. 161).

Some shorter works devoted to *CY* are Allen Guttman's "Mark Twain's *Connecticut Yankee:* Affirmation of the Vernacular Tradition?," which claims that Twain did *not* identify with Hank; rather, that "The Boss represents a turning-point in the hard road from ill-founded optimism to starkest nihilism." In "The Once and Future Boss: Mark Twain's Yankee," Chadwick Hansen,

found his "true vocation" in the great Colt arms factory where, surrounded by the tools of violence, he fights his way to a superintendentship. Set apart from the men under him by his position as foreman, Hank is not modest about the abilities that earned him his rank: "I could make anything a body wanted —anything in the world," he boasts (*CY*, p. 20). His aggressiveness also earns him the enmity of the "rough men" he supervises, however, and it is through one of their fights that he receives the blow that sends him backward in time.

Hank, then, differs from de Conte and August in that he is an adult from the modern era rather than a boy from the medieval and in that he serves as both narrator and focal character in the novel. Nevertheless, Hank, like the boys, is not entirely comfortable about his status. He differs from August and de Conte less in the problem he faces than in the way he handles it. Despite his bravado, being considered a deviation from the norm clearly disturbs him, and his insistence on his superiority —his constant need to assert it in Camelot as he had asserted it in Hartford—is both a response to finding himself regarded as an alien and a cause of the prolongation of his uncomfortable state. In other words, Hank begins his sojourn in the sixth century being regarded as an anomaly, and although he does not like his isolation, he deliberately exacerbates it. He chooses *not* to try to

---

reading twentieth-century theories of the authoritarian personality back into Twain's work, sees Hank as a dictator who might "celebrate the people in the abstract . . . and yet respond to actual persons with contempt, hatred, and . . . distrust"; while Judith Fetterley, in "Yankee Showman and Reformer: The Character of Mark Twain's Hank Morgan," *Texas Studies in Language and Literature*, sees the Yankee as an egotist who, as a would-be reformer, "turns into the world's greatest evil." Finally, in "The Meaning of *A Connecticut Yankee*," a recent revisionist reading of the novel, Everett Carter uses E. D. Hirsch's definition of authorial intent to contend, "The meaning of the work is a defense of the American nineteenth century [rather] than the reverse" (p. 425).

Hank's attack on institutions—his reflection of Mark Twain's political stances—concerns this study far less than does Hank's reflection of Mark Twain's psychological stances. It seems to me that Hank's sense of himself as an outsider is a sign of *consistency* in Mark Twain's work: while Hank's political stances fluctuate, his sense of uneasiness—except during his idyll with wife and child—does not. Hank celebrates labor and derides hereditary rule in one chapter but celebrates firm government and derides human "muck" in the next. Clearly he distrusts any kind of rule except his own; his need to "boss this asylum" may rest on his sense that he is the only one who can create any kind of rational order in the worlds in which he finds himself.

become an invisible member of the society because, on the one hand, he sees his transportation through time as a glorious opportunity to rule a kingdom and, on the other, he does not want to identify himself with a society whose values he so vehemently rejects.

As he had become foreman in Connecticut through talent and brawn, Hank becomes The Boss in England through talent and gall. His ostensibly modest claim that he wants his title from the people does not in the least way negate the fact that he still wants a title; he just wants confirmation of his superiority from everyone concerned. De Conte is born a nobleman; August earns professional rank; Hank schemes to have nobility thrust upon him—and he succeeds. All use social caste to distinguish themselves from the other characters. For Hank this is a means of confirming that he is not only different (a fact clear to everyone in the kingdom) but better—better than the born nobility because he is smarter and has earned his titles; better than the common people because they say he is, and acknowledge it by their spontaneous gesture of "electing" him The Boss. For Hank democratic leadership is universal agreement that he is the one genius in a society of equals. He values the mark of distinction, not the people's love. "There were very few THE's," he tells us proudly, "and I was one of them" (*CY*, p. 103). As neither commoner nor nobleman he can feel superior to both and can act independently of class affiliations; most importantly, he can persuade himself that he is indispensable to the evolution of the society.

Although Hank responds to his predicament by seeking mastery, he quickly learns how lonely the top can be. Being both narrator and central character of his story, he can display his sense of isolation more effectively than could either August or de Conte, both of whom began their stories at least nominally sharing the values of their culture. As an intruder into the sixth century, Hank has no reason to accept any of the Catholic world's premises; he is consequently the "only" nonbeliever until he (apparently) wins Clarence over to his side. Although he uses his alien status as a lever to effect reform, he never ceases to feel uncomfortable about being a stranger, even when he has gained more real power than anyone else in the kingdom.

Unlike 44, he is always intensely aware of the way other people regard him. He indicates his uneasiness as soon as he arrives in Camelot: "All of these people stared at me . . . but nobody even noticed that other fellow," he remarks when the mounted knight brings him into the confines of the city (*CY*, p. 28). Consequently, he queries his neighbors in an "insinuating, confidential way," hoping someone will confirm his hypothesis that he has woken up in an insane asylum. Eventually, his "consciousness," though not his "reason," urges him to believe Clarence's claim that he is in Camelot: "I seemed to believe the boy, I didn't know why. *Something* in me seemed to believe him—my consciousness, as you may say; but my reason didn't" (*CY*, p. 35). And he finally accepts what he cannot understand: "In the stillness and the darkness, realization soon began to supplement knowledge" (*CY*, p. 71).

Perhaps Hank's aggressive need to "boss this asylum" has as much to do with his sense of being an alien as with anything else. "The way I was looked upon was odd, but it was natural," he remarks:

> I had no pedigree, no inherited title; so in the king's and nobles' eyes I was mere dirt; the people regarded me with wonder and awe, but there was no reverence mixed with it; through the force of inherited ideas they were not able to conceive of anything being entitled to that except pedigree and lordship. (*CY*, p. 100)

It is precisely those "inherited ideas" that Hank attacks; although he claims to have made peace with what he calls "my anomalous position in King Arthur's kingdom," there is a stridency to his voice that belies his indifference. When he compares himself to the people around him as "a master intelligence among intellectual moles," he indicates how he really feels about being regarded as "that kind of elephant." Like August Feldner, he may despise those about him, but he dislikes having *them* despise *him*. While August fears ostracism, however, Hank turns it to his advantage, using it as a means of mastery rather than regarding it as a weakness. When he is first transported into Arthurian England, he thinks, in a fashion typical among Twain's characters when they feel disoriented, that he is dreaming. Furthermore, his experience of dreams reflects Twain's suspicion that they represent an alternative reality rather than imaginative ephemera: "I knew by past experience of the life-like intensity of dreams, that to be burned to death, even in a dream, would be very far from being a jest," Hank exclaims (*CY*, p. 62). Yet he masters this dream world as he earlier had mastered his waking one in New England, by converting his new environment into a challenge to his ingenuity: "I saw that I was just another Robinson Crusoe cast away on an uninhabited island, with no society but some more or less tame animals, and if I wanted to make life bearable I must do as he did—invent, contrive, create, reorganize things; set brain and hand to work, and keep them busy. Well, that was in my line" (*CY*, p. 85).

Thus, while August's response to hostility is to hide (either within himself or in the cellar of the castle), Hank's is to master his enemies, and while August relies on 44 to introduce change, Hank sees himself as a latter-day Prometheus. Once he accepts his situation, Hank claims to be "just as much at home in that century as I could have been in any other" (*CY*, p. 95); although he initially laments the fact that "I shall never see my friends again" (*CY*, p. 35), it would appear that his only real intimate had been a telephone operator whom he remembers talking to but never mentions having met face to face. Despite his claim to miss her, her real importance to him may lie in the fact that her response to his call of "Hello-Central" epitomizes the technological society he has lost. Yet that society, while providing the comforts of technology, only gave him a chance to boss a factory, while Arthurian England, he suddenly realizes, gives him a chance to boss the realm.

The other major reason Hank wants to maintain his distance from his new environment is that despite his claim to lack "sentiment," he is outraged by the culture's cruelty, especially in regard to its treatment of peasant families. While he does lack the extraordinary sensitivity that made de Conte the "only one" pure enough to hear Joan's prophecies or August the only one capable of sympathizing with the tortured Stranger, Hank's sensitivity to human suffering is as fully developed as theirs, and the sight of people in pain moves him to eloquence as well as to anger. When a young mother, condemned to the stake for petty thievery, receives assurance that her baby will be cared for, Hank's response belies his claim to a lack of poetry: "You should have seen her face then!" he exclaims. "Gratitude? Lord, what do you want with words to express that? Words are only painted fire; a look is the fire itself" (*CY*, p. 464). In addition, his respect for Arthur's act of risking his own life to care for a family dying of smallpox stimulates one of his rare encomiums: "Here was heroism at its last and loftiest possibility, its utmost summit; this was challenging death in the open field unarmed, with all the odds against the challenger, no reward set upon the contest, and no admiring world in silks and cloth of gold to gaze and applaud. . . . He was great now, sublimely great" (*CY*, p. 372).

Hank's sensitivity to suffering—and, interestingly, to psychological as well as to physical torture—is the factor that makes him so determined to destroy Morgan le Fay's power. His campaign against the legal system is largely motivated by his perception of the consequences that individuals' crimes had for their families: "The bitter law takes the convicted man's estate and beggars his widow and his orphans" (*CY*, p. 212). He lauds a peasant who endures the rack without confessing his crime because he does it in order to save his wife and child from being evicted: "They could torture you to death, but without conviction or confession they could not rob your wife and baby. You stood by them like a man; and *you*—true wife and woman that you are—you would have brought him release from torture at cost to yourself of slow starvation and death—well, it humbles a body to think what your sex can do when it comes to self-sacrifice" (*CY*, p. 212). He is infuriated by Le Fay's plot to torture one prisoner by staging funerals at his home and placing him in a cell from which he could see the funeral preparations—but not make out which of his relatives remained. Certainly the sum of physical and spiritual suffering that Hank sees is what leads him to conclude that "all France could hardly contain the coffins filled by that older and real Terror—that unspeakably bitter and awful Terror which none of us has been taught to see in its vastness or pity as it deserves" (*CY*, p. 157).

Since there is no question that Hank's story is narrated by a stranger to the society in which he finds himself, and since he does not hesitate to condemn the injustices he perceives, literacy does not function as an additional tool for his own estrangement from medieval culture. In August's and de Conte's development, literacy is the particular factor that forces them to analyze their society in the process of recording the reactions of the people about them to the extraordinary creature in their midst. Since Hank *is* the extraordinary creature, his dual function as narrator and protagonist does not engender conflict between his loyalties to the culture and to the truth. Rather, his analysis of the society is natural to his role as observer of a people who are as strange to him as he is to them.

Nevertheless, literacy plays a definite role in this novel, one similar to the role we have seen it play before. From the time the Yankee realizes that "nobody in the country could read or write but a few dozen priests" (*CY*, p. 87), he makes literacy and denominational freedom the cornerstone of his civilization: "I had started a teacher-factory and a lot of Sunday-schools the first thing; and as a result, I now had an admirable system of graded schools in full blast in those places, and also a complete variety of Protestant congregations all in a prosperous and growing condition" (*CY*, p. 118). In good Protestant fashion, Hank associates literacy and denominational choice with freedom from slavery to "inherited ideas," perhaps because for him, as for other nineteenth-century Protestants, literacy is associated with an individual's ability to read and interpret the Bible for himself and thus serves as a defense against the dogmatism of the Church. August and the young de Conte, though reticent about openly criticizing the Church, learned to doubt its precepts during their evolution into observers and recorders; Hank hopes to train the "brightest young minds" in England to such a degree of scientific skepticism that they will help him to destroy the power of the Church altogether. In preparation he spreads "confidential agents" throughout the country "to gnaw a little at this and that and the other superstition" (*CY*, p. 120). His branch schools and his military and naval academies are part of this scheme, as are his regional newspapers and the knights who roam the realm carrying sandwich boards with advertisements painted on them. Hank hopes all these agents will effect the changes in consciousness he needs before he can explode the "serene volcano" he has created under the Church's nose. He understands that literacy is the basis of revolutions, and at the end of his tenure in office the most subversive people in the kingdom are those he has trained to read, write, and think for themselves.[2]

Yet the freedom from inherited ideas that literacy has helped these people attain is also the agency for their estrangement and death just as it had been for August and de Conte. Those two narrators function officially as observers rather than as protagonists, and they demonstrate the protagonists' effects upon them through their own intellectual growth. In *A Connecticut Yankee*, however, we have to see through Hank's egocentrism to glimpse his effect on the boys whom he "reforms." The plights of Clarence, Hank's aide, and the fifty-two boys whom he has chosen to help defend their fortress more clearly illustrate how literacy can alienate its possessors from their peers than the plight of Hank, a stranger from another era, can ever do. Aware that they have abandoned the community in which they were born and have forfeited their claim to a place in their own culture, the boys—who apparently no longer even speak the same idiom as their contemporaries—try to articulate the dilemma their new allegiance has posed for them. Hank records that when they, "in the neat modern English . . . taught in my schools," express their concern that their own people are leagued against them, they tell him, "Our minds approve, but our hearts reproach us. . . . Oh, sir, consider! —reflect! —these

2. It is generally accepted that Twain's anti-Catholicism was part of his suspicion of the coercive power of any superstructure with control over men's hearts and minds. I am sure that his fear of the Church was also a half-conscious legacy from his Midwest Protestant background. In hating the Church for its massive political force and its ideological distortion of what he considered to be the real world, Twain proves his affinity with most other American intellectuals of his day, from James Fenimore Cooper to Francis Parkman. The movement from distrusting the Roman Church to protesting the dominance of any church was also a part of the prevailing creed, but the protest itself, paradoxically enough, became part of the ideological material for an American establishment. In "The Role of Religion in the Revolution," William McLoughlin offers a detailed analysis of the development of the ideology of religious liberty as a means of establishing a Protestant Christian nation. According to him, "free enterprise" among Protestant denominations helped cement the country's new self-image and, ironically, thus became a part of the new establishment. The rhetoric of this ideology quickly passed into the common language, becoming a part of America's missionary nationalism. Certainly it is legitimate for Hank Morgan, in his role as the American reformer, to use it as a basis for seeking to

people are our people, they are bone of our bone, flesh of our flesh, we love them—do not ask us to destroy our nation!" (*CY*, p. 552).

Despite the fact that Hank persuades them that they will be fighting the military, not the populace, the words they speak are true. Furthermore, Hank secretly knows it, for, anticipating their plea, he tells us that he has prepared an answer "well chosen and tranquilizing"(*CY*, p. 552)—tranquilizing enough to send them voluntarily to their deaths.[3] The boys' forfeiture of a place in their own century is the reason Clarence, the boy first converted and the one most loyal to Hank's cause, is the most appropriate character to end the tale; not only has he lost a place in his own time, he is the one most sensitive to the insolubility of their problem and most able to articulate it. He, not Hank, understands that Hank cannot "educate the superstition out of those people"; his perception is the result of his dual participation in the mentality of both Hank's culture and his own.

When Hank is enchanted by Merlin, Clarence finishes his narrative for him, but although he completes his brief summary

---

replace Arthur and the Church's establishment with his own new multidenominational establishment.

3. The blood and gore of the Battle of the Sand Belt have disturbed recent critics more than any other incident in *Connecticut Yankee*, perhaps because they have seen our own recent history in Hank's apparent relish for the destruction his technological genius wreaks. Guttman, in "Mark Twain's *Connecticut Yankee*," claims that Hank's "technological utopia becomes a holocaust," and Hank "exults over the strewn dead" (p. 105); in a footnote Hansen, in "The Once and Future Boss," compares Hank to Adolf Hitler (pp. 66–67). In *Mark Twain: An American Prophet*, Geismar claims that "the fantasy of mass killing by scientific machines, of instantaneous destruction, had superseded the earlier dream" (p. 124). Blues, who thinks Mark Twain feared and distrusted the isolated individual, sees Twain's inability to bring Hank back into the community as the structural problem at the heart of *Connecticut Yankee* and cites the Battle of the Sand Belt as evidence of Twain's realization that the "magician of science cannot rise above his selfish desires for adulation and power . . . he becomes . . . an ominous symbol of 'modern technological man' " (*Mark Twain and the Community*, p. 52). On the other hand, Everett Carter, in "The Meaning of *A Connecticut Yankee*," simply holds that the carnage at the end is "no aberration, but a conventional mode of frontier hyperbole" (p. 430). Although I am disturbed by the violence of the Battle, I find myself equally disturbed by Hank's assumption that the boys for whom he is responsible should be willing to remain pariahs among their own people merely out of loyalty to him and to his ideals. This assumption—perhaps unconscious even on Twain's part—as much as any other assumption in the novel, strikes me as evidence of the arrogance of the American imperialist.

of the little army's last days in the cave, he apparently does not survive the debacle Hank has brought about: "As for the rest of us," he writes, "well, it is agreed that if any one of us ever escapes alive from this place, he will write the fact here, and loyally hide this Manuscript with the Boss, our dear good chief, whose property it is, be he alive or dead" (*CY*, p. 571). As no name is recorded we assume that one escaped. Hank's meddling in the boys' lives has removed the possibility of their ever resuming a place in their own culture; they die in the cave where Hank lies in enchanted sleep, while he, in an ironic inversion of the Arthur myth, "lives" to yearn for death, for escape, from "the torture of those hideous dreams" that haunt him when he awakes back in the nineteenth century (*CY*, p. 574). Because Clarence dies a "lasting" death he is spared the nightmare of returning to life in an era no longer his own, and he thus achieves the extinction of consciousness for which Hank later claims to long.

Although Hank more often tries to deal with his anxieties by looking for ways to manipulate the people he distrusts than by looking for symbols of spiritual solace, during his sojourn in the sixth century he unexpectedly discovers a means of spiritually transcending his conflicts with his social environment. The intensity with which he has viewed familial love and female self-abnegation throughout the novel stems in part from his Victorian ideas about the hearth and home, but also from his bachelor state. Hank The Boss is—especially in Arthurian England—lonely. Thus, when he marries Sandy, the girl who accompanies him on his adventure in knight errantry, she ceases to be presented as a comic character and evolves into the Victorian ideal of the good wife, while he, in turn, becomes a responsible husband and father. Most importantly, after he marries, Hank learns that mistrust may not be the only mode of psychological existence; rather, he discovers that hearth and home can be a spiritual sanctuary in an otherwise antagonistic human landscape.

Perhaps more than any other of Twain's narratives, *A Connecticut Yankee* demonstrates the importance that domestic security assumed in the nineteenth century as a substitute for status security.[4] Hank originally claims that he has married Sandy "for no particular reason except that by the customs of chivalry she was my property . . . I was a New Englander, and in my opinion this sort of partnership would compromise her, sooner or later" (*CY*, pp. 523–24). In other words, Hank originally sees his act as a contractual rather than an emotional matter, a compromise between his Victorian morals and his medieval circumstances. Eventually, however, the marriage functions to give him a sense of emotional security that no other situation conveys.

"In my dreams, along at first," Hank records of the early days of his marriage, "I still wandered thirteen centuries away, and my unsatisfied spirit went calling and harking all up and down the unreplying vacancies of a vanished world" (*CY*, p. 524). Like many Victorians, Hank's dream life reveals his longing for a certainty of time and place that neither the technological sterility of the society he has left nor the absolutism of the Church he rejects can supply him. Since he talks in his sleep, Hank's sense of loss is disclosed to his wife, whose response is to name their child "Hello-Central," a word she understands to be the name of a lover left behind. Hello thus represents the fusion of Hank's two worlds; as his offspring she illustrates a degree of intimacy that he apparently never achieved in his first life, where the telephone stood between him and his girl; as a reminder of the

4. The Victorian image of the family—hearth and home—evolved in inverse proportion to the decline of certainty in both the social and the religious realm. As the world beyond the house became increasingly one of flux—whether because of business cycles or because of the onslaught of scientific skepticism —it became increasingly difficult to find a stable social, financial, or theological "place." The increasing attention paid to creation of a warm—even, aesthetically, enveloping—domestic environment was one response to this crisis. Certainly Clemens's Hartford home, large, convoluted, stuffed with comfortable furniture, enclosing a small conservatory (one did not even have to go outside to experience nature) and having few windows, is evidence of a desire to pull back from the "outside" world into an inner one. The cult of the family, including the children's dominance as centers of attention, was practiced without reserve in that house. As Twain was writing *Connecticut Yankee* the first cracks in that familial armor were beginning to appear; many critics have pointed to his financial overinvestment in the Paige typesetter at that time as part of the animus behind the satire directed at Hank's technological destructiveness. See, for one instance, James M. Cox, "*A Connecticut Yankee in King Arthur's Court:* The Machinery of Self-Preservation." When Hank finds peace with Sandy and Hello he finds peace with the rest of the society; this "center-

technology that produced the telephone, she reminds him of his civilizing "mission." Most importantly, she is that rare being in American novels, the protagonist's child, his physical legacy to the future and his proof that he is contributing to the community. Hank is so involved with Sandy and Hello that concern for the baby's health causes the hitherto impossible: he becomes "unconscious of any world outside of that sick-room" (*CY*, p. 526). The baby, he tells us, is "the centre of the universe," and marriage he terms "the dearest and perfectest comradeship that ever was."

Thus, as a husband and father Hank transcends his sense of embattlement; the emotional stability his new status yields functions to transform his relationship to the rest of the society. Lancelot assumes the role of a kindly uncle, the knights of the Round Table become a baseball team, the castle figures as the structure that contains the nursery, and Hank tells us that he is "very happy" (*CY*, p. 571). Before he marries, both the sixth and the nineteenth centuries mean the same thing to him; they are time spans in which he battles for survival in a world that seems to yield no provision for psychic tranquillity. His previous responses to the destruction of nuclear families were clues to the importance this seemingly incorrigible bachelor attached to the family, and now marriage stabilizes him emotionally; his family becomes more important than power struggles, and his antagonists become actors in the evolution of a domestic drama. Directing his energies toward the creation of a tranquil environment rather than toward the destruction of medieval values, he discovers a center of consciousness that alleviates his loneliness. Consequently, when he lies dying thirteen hundred years later and thinks, in his delirium, that Sandy is near him, his face lights up "with pleasure, gratitude, gladness, welcome," the framing narrator records, and he cries that "all is peace, and I am happy again" (*CY*, p. 573). In his delirium Sandy and the sixth century seem to be his "real" life and the nineteenth century the dream: "I seemed to have flown back out of that age into this of ours," he tells his phantom wife, "and then forward to it again, and was set down, a stranger and forlorn, in that strange

---

ing" in the novel reflects Twain's sense that only the family provides stability at the "heart" of an otherwise chaotic world.

England, with an abyss of thirteen centuries yawning between me and you! between me and my home and my friends! between me and all that is dear to me, all that could make life worth the living!" (*CY*, p. 574). The sixth century has become his home because it contains the figure of wife and child and the security that these images suggest to a mentality more accustomed to suspicion and hostility than to trust and contentment.

Hank's respite, however, is brief. Forced to leave his family in France and return to the battleground of England, his adventure in the sixth century ends with the Battle of the Sand Belt. When he returns to the nineteenth century, the framing narrator tells us, he is "old, old, unspeakably old and faded and dry and musty and ancient" (*CY*, p. 17), haunted by his "fantastic frenzy of . . . dreams" (*CY*, p. 574). He dies in the throes of a fancied battle; despite his illusion that Sandy is with him, clearly his spirit is no longer at ease. Dan Beard's illustration for this page suggests a reunion in heaven, but Mark Twain's narrative is pointedly devoid of one; it seems likely that having lost both his public power and his private sanctuary, and at home neither in the nineteenth century nor in the sixth, Hank—much like August—is doomed to be alone in "the pathetic drift between the centuries" forever.

A Connecticut Yankee in King Arthur's Court was completed some twenty-five years before "No. 44, The Mysterious Stranger,"[5] and it is clear that Twain had not yet arrived at the desperate solipsism that the later book reveals. Nevertheless, it, too, concerns a character who, like 44, can move from one era to another and who, like August, sees his limited freedom from temporality as a means to effect fundamental changes in the chain of human events. It is generally agreed that one of the "flaws" of *A Connecticut Yankee* is that Hank repeatedly changes his opinion of human nature: he fluctuates between affirming that "a man *is* a man, at bottom. Whole ages of abuse and oppression cannot crush the manhood out of him" (*CY*, p. 390) and swearing that "I was ashamed of the whole human

5. Probably early in 1889. See Albert Bigelow Paine, *Mark Twain: A Biography*, 2:887ff.

race" (*CY*, p. 246). [6] Hank's philosophical flipflops reveal Twain in a period of radical uncertainty; even Albert Bigelow Paine, who tends to play down Twain's misanthropy, admits that in the 1880s Twain was replacing his pleasure in human foibles with a progressive disdain for human stupidity. [7] Fred Lorch has explored the possibility that *A Connecticut Yankee* was initially conceived as a book about the effects of environment, especially of religious training, on the shape of individual lives and that Twain first located it on the Sandwich Islands. [8] The completed novel substitutes a community removed in time for one removed in space and can be seen as an almost Zolaesque experiment in reforming human nature through reforming the human environment. As such, it proves the null hypothesis. Hank utilizes his displacement in time to attempt reform "at the dawn of western civilization" only to find that at the root of human error lies human evil itself.

As a sociologist, then, Hank discovers that a man's cultural background is not the only factor determining his actions. More importantly for our purposes, Hank's record of his emotional responses to his discoveries shows how central the image of domesticity was for a man threatened by forces that at any moment could move beyond his control. A nonconformist in all societies, and constantly fighting to master his situation in the public sphere, Hank finds repose only in the figures of wife and child and the tiny community they represent. With them he

6. Hank's conflicting pronouncements are the source of much of the critical schism over the meaning of *Connecticut Yankee:* those who, like Louis J. Budd or Everett Carter, think the novel demonstrates Twain's continued faith in human perfectionism choose to cite Hank's environmentalist statements; those who, like Henry Nash Smith, think it demonstrates Twain's growing pessimism cite Hank's determinist ones. Others, myself included, agree with Roger B. Salomon that Twain "wavered between two propositions" in *Connecticut Yankee:* that "man was either born innately good and made bad, or born innately bad and could be trained to be better" (*Twain and the Image of History,* p. 95). I find *Connecticut Yankee* the first of Twain's novels to *overtly* exhibit his emerging pessimism: the view, in Howard Baetzhold's terms, "that the basic nature of the human race provided a formidable . . . obstacle" to reform (*Mark Twain and John Bull,* p. 161). Moreover, I think Hank's philosophical ambivalence is a direct reflection of the daily reversals of his creator.

7. See Paine, *Biography,* 2:887ff. This is a theme Paine develops slowly—and reluctantly—in vol. 2.

8. Fred W. Lorch, "Hawaian Feudalism and Mark Twain's *Connecticut Yankee.*"

withstands the hostility he feels directed against him; without them he feels he must continually prove himself. Even when he is happy and successful in Arthur's court, he is always conscious of the precariousness of his position. Moreover, without Sandy and Hello he is lonely; like de Conte and August, his inability to share the values of the society in which he finds himself suspends him in an emotional no-man's-land. Unlike de Conte, however, the immortality he achieves does not promise redemption; rather, like August he lives, in solitary agony, through his displacement in space and time.

4

Adventures of Huckleberry Finn: Huck Finn

You must become an ignorant man again
And see the sun again with an ignorant eye
And see it clearly in the idea of it.
                    —Wallace Stevens

As we have seen, the term *alienation* is used in this study to describe the uneasiness a character feels when he realizes that he cannot wholly share the value system of a given group. In the novels we have examined so far, narrative alienation was manifested consciously, either, as with Hank Morgan, as an overt rejection of the values of an alien culture, or, as with Louis de Conte, as a gradual process of psychological disengagement from one's own culture. Whether the narrators begin or end their narratives with indications that they are not comfortable in their social group, at some point they all do assume an antagonistic stance. All indicate the loneliness that their spiritual independence engenders, and all find respite from it through preferred images that enable them to feel that there is some ideal "place" where they can feel truly at "home," that is, unselfconsciously at ease.

It is rather more difficult to discuss Huckleberry Finn in terms of narrative alienation than it is to discuss de Conte, August, and Hank because, first, the concept strikes many readers as absurdly incongruous with Huck's naiveté and, second, Huck almost never makes a directly antagonistic statement about his society. Nevertheless, Huck does communicate a nervousness, a tension, that is central to his narrative stance. Huck's alienation is more complex than that of the other narrators because in part it is a result of class differences: as the town pariah, child of the town drunkard, he has developed an outsider's point of view because he has been treated like an outsider all his life. But Huck's tensions also spring from his moral

60

consciousness. Like the other narrators we have examined, he imposes psychic distance between himself and others because he cannot tolerate the way they treat one another. Even though he shares many of the culture's assumptions, he is in fundamental—if largely unconscious—disagreement with the hypocrisy and cruelty that characterize the lives of his neighbors. Yet he has too weak a sense of his own moral rectitude to criticize others outright. When he finds himself in conflict, he assumes that he, rather than they, is wrong. Thus the famous "dramatic irony" of *Huckleberry Finn*, the narrative strategy whereby the author forces the reader, more sophisticated than the narrator, to make judgments the narrator cannot. In *Adventures of Huckleberry Finn* the reader is an accomplice of the novel's didactic intent. The hermeneutical structure of the book mandates that we do Huck's moralizing for him.

By discussing *Adventures of Huckleberry Finn* (1884) last, I hope to show how the pattern of Huck's conflict with his society and his escape to the tranquillity of the river conforms to the patterns of alienation and resolution in the other texts already examined. Clearly, in *Huckleberry Finn* the river is the place where Huck feels most comfortable; by analyzing his descriptions we will better understand how the timelessness of the river landscape is central to the ideal landscape of Mark Twain's preferred images. Prior to examining Huck's patterns of resolution, however, it will be useful to briefly review Huck's patterns of alienation, first, because they are similar to the distancing exhibited by de Conte and August (if not by Hank); second, because one of the effects of *Huckleberry Finn*'s unique narrative strategy is to make the reader experience Huck's ecstasies in the same way he or she experiences Huck's anxieties. By making us perceive as Huck does, the author pulls us into Huck's center of consciousness.

As in the other patterns of alienation we have examined, in *Huck Finn* literacy functions as a means of separating Huck from the people to whom he has the closest connections. In contrast to the society of the Middle Ages, Huck's society values literacy: on the American frontier it was regarded as one of the dividing lines between primitive and civilized men. In *Adventures of Huckleberry Finn* even the con men are marginally literate, gaining their livelihood in part through bringing makeshift scenes from Shakespeare's plays to the culture-starved inhabitants of the river towns, while Tom Sawyer, who is often seen as epitomizing the society, is not merely literate but widely read and an active thief of literary ideas for use in his adventures. Although Huck initially resists learning to read, once he realizes that education will make him different from Pap, he begins to regard education favorably. For all his resistance to "respectability" Huck is enough a product of his society not to want to be classed with its dregs. Thus, when Pap invades his room at the Widow's and insists that Huck stop going to school because "Your mother couldn't read, and she couldn't write, nuther, before she died. None of the family couldn't, before *they* died. *I* can't; and here you're a-swelling yourself up like this" (*HF*, p. 18, Twain's emphasis), Huck recalls that "I didn't want to go to school much, before, but I reckoned I'd go now to spite pap" (*HF*, p. 21). While on the one hand Huck's attitude can be seen simply as rebellion against his father, it is also his way of distancing himself. By rejecting Pap's values, he demonstrates that he is better than his drunken, thieving sire.

Literacy also helps Huck convince himself that even though he and Jim are friends, he is still different from the slave not only because he is white but also because he is smarter. Most of his conflict about their relationship comes from the fact that a "nigger lover" is rated a step below "trash" in his society, and while he never forgets their racial difference, as his intimacy with Jim progresses he runs the risk of forgetting that it matters. One of the ways in which he reminds himself that he and Jim are different and that he, being white, must be correct, is to read to Jim out of the books they salvage from the wreck of the *Walter Scott* and to stand by written authority even when Jim presents the commonsense objections to conventional wisdom that, in other contexts, Huck would usually have presented himself. As he realized that he could establish social distance from Pap by learning to read, so he also establishes intellectual and emotional distance from Jim by demonstrating the one skill he has that Jim—his superior in almost every other useful art—does not possess. In both cases literacy is a tool for him to define his difference from the two men with whom he has the most in common and who have the strongest legal and moral claims on him.

While he uses literacy to indicate his superiority to Pap and Jim, Huck uses his unworthiness to indicate his inferiority to others. His class consciousness, in other words, is a tool for him to establish distance. Even when he is approached by a person sincerely willing to grant him membership in society, he creates barriers by insisting that he is undeserving. Despite wanting to please the Widow by accepting her God, for example, he insists, "I couldn't make out how he [God] was agoing to be any better off than what he was before, seeing I was so ignorant and so kind of low-down and ornery" (*HF*, pp. 11–12). Throughout his sojourn with the Widow he tries to convince himself that, as Miss Watson claims, "I was a fool." In implying that he is unworthy to belong to civilized society he gives himself an excuse to leave it; in an almost Emersonian effort to preserve his independence, he defines all people he encounters as antitheses to himself.

Huck establishes distance from the more respectable members of the community less purposefully than he does from Pap or Jim, as an almost reflexive response to his intuition that their values differ from his own. His uneasiness about the community—the "special sensitivity" Thomas Blues sees as at the root of much of Huck's defensiveness—is marked by the same raw sensitivity to hypocrisy, cruelty, and violence demonstrated by de Conte, August, and Hank. As Twain uses the ideology of the Church in the three novels we have already examined, in *Huckleberry Finn* he uses the ideology of slavery as a means of showing how severely a web of false values can warp human morals and how keenly Huck's sensibility (if not his rationality) responds to moral decadence. It is generally recognized that in this novel Jim, as the representative victim of slavery, is the touchstone for morality; virtually every character is evaluated in regard to him or another slave, and only Huck and Mary Jane Wilks demonstrate any degree of sensitivity to his plight. But while slavery is the historically correct catalyst for the demonstration of human evil in *Huckleberry Finn*, it is not the only one. Humaneness is measured not only by the responses of white people to black ones but by their responses to each other as well; their lack of humaneness is proved to transcend racial categories and provides the implicit justification for Huck's nervousness whenever he encounters a new group.[1]

Huck's responses to the inhabitants of Bricksville, to the Grangerford and Shepardson feud, and to the King and the Duke have been subjected to much critical analysis and do not need extensive review here.[2] Nevertheless, it is useful to note that his

---

1. The critical controversy about Huck's attitude toward his society is far less vehement than that about Hank Morgan's; however, while everyone agrees that Huck is uneasy around "Shore People," to use Henry Nash Smith's term, they are not agreed over the degree to which Huck "rejects" the values of his society. A sampling of recent views illustrates typical similarities and differences. Thomas Blues, for instance, feels that Twain thwarted Huck's incipient anarchism when he brought him back into the fold during the Phelps episode (*Mark Twain and the Community*, pp. 19–21), but Maxwell Geismar feels that Huck Finn *"defied* all the proprieties, including . . . wealth, success, social position, and conventional religion" (*Mark Twain: An American Prophet*, p. 87). Analyzing Twain's style, in *Mark Twain: The Development of a Writer*, Henry Nash Smith claims that Huck's and Jim's flight "obviously translates into action the theme of vernacular protest" (p. 115), and Robert Regan, in *Unpromising Heroes: Mark Twain and His Characters*, sees Mark Twain as "at pains to emphasize the false, the dishonest, and the hypocritical side of St. Petersburg life" (p. 135). In *The Art of Mark Twain*, William Gibson, too, sees the "continual drama of foolish and ferocious citizens . . . 'the damned human race' " as "a second major motif" in the novel (p. 113); and James M. Cox, in "Toward Vernacular Humor," *The Virginia Quarterly Review* 46 (Spring 1970): 311–30, sees Huck's "rejection of civilization" at the end of the book as "the radically negative vision which his doubly negative grammar embodies." Moreover Alan Trachtenburg, in "The Form of Freedom in *Huckleberry Finn*," *The Southern Review* 6 (October 1970): 954–71, sees Huck's conflict with his society as one of "conformity versus autonomy." The crucial point, for all readers, rests on Huck's assumption that he, rather than the society, is wrong, and the argument concerns to what degree this constitutes "rejection." With those critics who view Huck's stance through an analysis of his style—Henry Nash Smith, Gladys Bellamy, James M. Cox, Alan Trachtenburg, and Richard Poirier, for instance—I feel that Huck's alienation from "Shore People" is implicit in his vernacular stance (that is, in his position as a character who is not conventionally "respectable") and in the metaphors through which he portrays what he sees.

2. The portrayal of human nature through the delimitation of the types of people Huck and Jim meet during their journey is the major reason most readers see *Adventures of Huckleberry Finn* as, in part, Mark Twain's criticism of pre-Civil War society and as a precursor of Twain's later invectives against "the damned human race." Again, a brief sampling of recent criticism should provide an overview of the whole. Believing that "Huck's socially anxious voice never carries fully the implications of social contempt and rejection that govern the metaphorical pattern of the book," Richard Poirier nevertheless believes that

responses parallel de Conte's horror at Joan's execution, August's anguish at an old woman's being burned at the stake, and Hank's outrage over the plight of England's slaves. In fact, the difference between Huck and these later narrators lies not in their response to human evil, but, as we have already noted, in the way they express it. Conscious of their narrative duties, the later narrators try to evaluate the behavior of the people they portray; the result is that, horrified by what they perceive, they openly moralize about it. Huck, in contrast, is neither a chronicler of a major historical event, a writer revealing his journey to enlightenment, nor a student of the social organism; consequently, he rarely, if ever, moralizes openly.[3] Since his stream-of-consciousness method of recording his experiences makes

"we are seeing in these repeated metaphors Mark Twain's own alienation from that society" (*A World Elsewhere: The Place of Style in American Literature*, pp. 152–53, 179–80). Smith, in *Mark Twain: The Development of a Writer*, claims that "the satire of the towns . . . insists . . . that the dominant culture is decadent and perverted" but that Huck's inability to respond openly detracts from his full development as a character (pp. 117–18). Geismar sees the "real form" of *Huckleberry Finn* as "a series of long, over-done, brutal . . . forays of 'civilization' . . . onto the raft" alternating with "the return into . . . a natural existence on the blessed raft" (*An American Prophet*, p. 96). Perhaps one of the most thorough of recent treatments of these episodes is in Gibson's *The Art of Mark Twain*, where he analyzes each episode as he shows that "in the second half of the novel Mark Twain plans primarily to illustrate life in small towns along the Mississippi" (p. 106) and that Huck's comment that "human beings *can* be awful cruel to one another" is a response to the great number of characters who "deserve damnation for their actions" (pp. 113–14).

3. The narrative irony of *Huckleberry Finn* is, for this reader, its most interesting stylistic aspect: critics who concentrate on Mark Twain's style have contributed to our understanding of it. Henry Nash Smith set the stage for this kind of analysis in the "Sound Heart and Deformed Conscience" chapter of *Development of a Writer*. James M. Cox may state the problem most clearly in *Mark Twain: The Fate of Humor*: "The vernacular . . . created the means of control within the reader's mind . . . first . . . Huck's incorrect language implied standard, correct, literary English. Second, Huck's status as a child invited an indulgence from the reader. Finally, Huck's action in time and place . . . ensured moral approval from the reader" (pp. 168–69). Trachtenburg, in "The Form of Freedom," also addresses this question, often in opposition to Smith; interested in the problem Mark Twain encountered in transforming oral into written art, Trachtenburg sees Huck's major mode of speaking as "deadpan," that is, as saying less than he means. Trachtenburg finds that this technical device thwarts Huck's full realization as a character, first, because he cannot be allowed to "know" what he means (which would destroy his naïveté), and second, because the deadpan voice precludes complete innocence. Both Cox and Trachtenburg throw the full realization of the moral intentions of the book back onto the reader; with this, if not with minor points, I am in full agreement.

him a transmitter rather than a translator of what he sees, however, one way of judging his response to experiences is to examine our own. As James Cox notes, "in turning the narration over to Huck, Mark Twain abandoned the explicit norms and risked making his vernacular force the reader to supply the implied norms."[4] Thus we see the "shackly dried-up frame concerns" that pass for houses in Bricksville, and the gardens that "didn't seem to raise anything in them but jimpson weeds, and sunflowers, and ash-piles, and old curled up boots" (*HF*, p. 117), and know that even though Huck never tells us that he thinks Bricksville is a decadent town, his description of a garden that only grows trash implicitly renders his evaluation. His metaphors tell us that Bricksville's residents are as worn-out morally as their environment is materially—they "roost" on dry-goods boxes and "lean" against awning posts. Even when he describes the delight the loafers take in "covering a dog with turpentine and seeing him run himself to death" (*HF*, p. 118), *he* avoids overt moralizing; nevertheless, by the standards of our culture the cruelty of the act is clear. Perhaps one reason *Adventures of Huckleberry Finn* is considered one of the most ethically concerned novels in our literature stems from the fact that Huck's narrative method elicits the reader's participation. By the time Huck, in one of his rare comments about the situation in which he is involved, remarks that "it was enough to make a body ashamed of the human race," readers have sufficiently participated in his experience to feel that he is reflecting their judgments rather than simply registering his own shock.

Not only do Huck's patterns of alienation demonstrate the same sensitivity to hypocrisy and cruelty that we have seen in the narratives of Louis de Conte, August Feldner, and Hank Morgan, his patterns of resolution are also familiar. The lyricism with which he records his experiences on the river alone with Jim echoes de Conte's paean to the fairy tree, Hank's to the institution of marriage, and August's dream-self's to his life in "general space"; most importantly, his portrayal of the experience indicates that for him it is an avenue to timelessness.

4. Cox, *The Fate of Humor*, p. 168.

Unlike the other narrators, however, Huck takes his readers with him through his escape from time. The narrative strategy of *Huckleberry Finn* permits us to share Huck's ecstasies much as it forces us to do his moralizing for him. Thus the same narrative precision that brings "pieces of bottles, and rags, and played-out tin ware" so vividly to our order-loving minds also brings "the branches . . . tossing their arms as if they was just wild" (*HF*, p. 42), or "the sky up there, all speckled with stars" (*HF*, p. 101) directly to our nature-starved sensibilities. Huck's preferred image is the river and the river landscape; as Richard Poirier notes, Huck's metaphors of the human landscape reflect the influence of Emerson's image of society as "a conspiracy . . . against the manhood of . . . its members," while Huck's metaphors of the natural landscape reflect the influence of Emerson's image of nature as the resting place for the self-reliant soul.[5]

One of the difficulties critics have always had in discussing Huck's narrative function stems from the fact that the very act of labeling it seems to distort Huck's posture. Most readers have settled for regarding him as a naif or new Adam; perhaps Poirier's perception that Huck's response to man and nature reflects Emersonian dualisms comes closest to the truth. In fact, Huck acts, in part, as a phenomenologist—a label that, in its pretensions to descriptive accuracy, is furthest from the boy's concept of himself. Yet Huck's inability to analyze, which implies that he has no sense of historical causation; his reluctance to moralize openly, which implies that he is not confident that he has a moral basis from which he can judge others; and, most importantly, his preference for precise physical details rather than for general statements, which implies that when he observes, he does so without the backlog of descriptive terminology that rules most verbal painters of landscapes, all function to bring him closer to the things he sees than any other of Twain's narrators. Consequently, in his stream-of-consciousness narration he functions phenomenologically, for in his extraordinarily precise descriptions, especially of the river landscape, he re-creates the objects of his perceptions with a sym-

5. Poirier, *A World Elsewhere*, pp. 150–51.

pathy that shows that he feels such an intimacy with the organic world that he virtually sees himself as part of it. Moreover, in rendering the river world as he perceives it he also re-creates—rather than simply recounts—his experience for the reader.[6]

Maurice Merleau-Ponty defines phenomenology, in part, as a philosophy that "places in abeyance the assertions arising out of the natural attitude, the better to understand them; but it is also a philosophy for which the world is always 'already there' before reflection begins—as an inalienable presence; and all its efforts are concentrated upon re-achieving a direct and primitive contact with the world and endowing that contact with a philosophical status."[7] The difference between a phenomenologist and a primitive is that the latter never arrives at the last step of Merleau-Ponty's formulation. Huck is a naif, not a philosopher; he certainly never endows his perceptions with any kind of status. Nevertheless—and the point, I think, is crucial—the last step in this phenomenological exercise is performed by the reader of *Adventures of Huckleberry Finn*, and any critic who comments on Huck's transcendental moments on the river has completed the philosophical task. When Huck portrays the landscape of the river he does not posit causes and effects (that is, he suspends the natural attitude); he merely describes the way it looks, feels, and sounds, and the reader is absorbed into the world he re-creates. When he describes how "the rain would thrash along so thick that the trees off a little ways looked dim and spider-webby" and how the thunder went "rumbling, grumbling, tumbling down the sky towards the other side of the world," we, too, hear and see the storm. Moreover, when he says that he "wouldn't want to be nowhere else but here," the nervousness he evinces in virtually all his contacts with others disappears. In these descriptions, he merges with, rather than distances himself from, the natural landscape. Consequently,

6. For a seminal account of Mark Twain's innovations in constructing Huck's landscape descriptions see Leo Marx, "The Pilot and the Passenger: Landscape Conventions and the Style of *Huckleberry Finn*." In "The Form of Freedom," Trachtenburg approaches my view of Huck's narrative function when he claims that our assessment of Huck's double role—as both actor and storyteller—"precedes assessment of the meaning of freedom" (p. 960).

7. Maurice Merleau-Ponty, "What Is Phenomenology?," p. 69.

when he reports that "days and nights swam by, they slid along so quiet and smooth and lovely" (*HF*, p. 99), he seems to speak from the timelessness of the diurnal cycle. Far from regarding nature as he regards society, as a "not-me" from which he seeks relief, he embraces the river landscape as his rightful home.

Thus in his lack of narrative consciousness, his *lack* of distance between himself and the objects of his perceptions, Huck Finn overcomes his sense of estrangement from the community and is fulfilled because he speaks from within the cycle of plenitude. His narrative strategy—his tendency to describe a scene so meticulously that the reader is absorbed in its detail and persuaded to do his or her own evaluation—recreates in the reader not only Huck's moments of unease but also his moments of joy. On the river Huck communicates his contentment in the process of describing the components of the immediate, sensory world in which he lives and with which he interacts; the effect of his narrative is to make the reader also retrieve that life-world as he or she reads his book. Huck's descriptions of his ecstatic moments actually let us experience what it feels like to be on the river through the immediacy of reading, or activating, the text. Part of his narrative function is to remind us that the sensory world exists beyond the narrow conventions of the human community and that it is the place for the regeneration of the soul.

Huckleberry Finn, then, is the only one of the narrators we have examined to have overcome his sense of estrangement from his society by finding an actual environment in which he can live both physically and spiritually. He is able to find it precisely because he is a naif; unlike the other narrators we have examined, he does not analyze, does not moralize, and does not reflect upon himself or the culture that seeks to control him; consequently, he neither asks the questions nor draws the conclusions that would cause him to reject the given world. Responding with the same sensitivity as the others to the same exhibitions of human depravity, he concludes that *he* is not fit for the community, rather than it for him. His very lack of egocentrism is the factor that saves him from despair; he does not feel that the community must be reformed because it does not conform to his expectations. Rather, he discovers a spiritual otherworld within the confines of the given one. Like the periods of respite experienced by the other narrators, Huck's experience of harmony with nature is fragile and intermittent, but while he is surrounded by the river, away from the world of men, he is happy. Instead of accepting his society's evaluations of the necessary and the good, he finds a landscape of spiritual repose and substitutes the plenitude of nature for the inadequacy of human relationships.

In a letter to his fiancée, Olivia Langdon, in 1868, Twain referred to "home" as "that type and symbol of heaven" from which he felt he was in exile, and he described his response as a "great blank," and "awful vacancy."[8] When he claimed that in visiting home he saw his family "taking delight in things that are new to me and which I do not comprehend," he was describing an emotional and temporal chasm that, to him, was as wide as the one Hank Morgan was later to perceive between himself and the nineteenth-century world to which he so reluctantly returned. It has often been noted that temporal and cultural distance represent emotional loss in Twain's work.[9] The narratives he sets in the Middle Ages seem more like science fiction than historical novels because the sense of alienation that rules their narrators' consciousness shows how distant they feel themselves to be from the historical contexts of their stories. These novels do not reconstruct the Middle Ages; rather, the narrators are so disaffected that they become the critics instead of the interpreters of their societies. As characters, they (like Clarence and his boys) find themselves with no nation to which they can return when they have completed their education. Spiritually afloat, as Twain phrased it in his letter to Livy, they drift between the centuries, searching for "that pillow of weariness, that refuge from care, and trouble, and pain . . . Home."[10] Yet each of these novels indicates that a spiritual refuge does

8. *Mark Twain's Collected Letters*, vol. 1, 1853–1869, edited by Lin Salamo, #251.

9. One of the broadest and most interesting discussions of this theme is Roger B. Salomon's "Realism as Disinheritance: Twain, Howells, and James."

10. *Mark Twain's Collected Letters*, vol. 1, 1853–1869, edited by Lin Salamo, #251.

exist, if only it can be located. In *Joan of Arc* it is evoked through a myth of innocence; in "No. 44, The Mysterious Stranger" through a brief vision of freedom from corporeality, in *A Connecticut Yankee* through association with a woman and child.

In *Huckleberry Finn*, the earliest written of these novels, the sense of drift that signals loneliness in the historical novels is transformed into Twain's most famous, and perhaps his own favorite, image of repose. Here the vacancy that exile from the community engenders is filled by the plenitude of nature: out on Jackson's Island, before he meets Jim, when Huck is lonely he goes and sits by the river because "there ain't no better way to put in the time when you are lonesome; you can't stay so, you soon get over it" (*HF*, p. 34). On the river the violence, selfishness, and death that Huck associates with the community are annulled by the continual transformation of one form of life into another, and Huck is joyous because he perceives life on the river as a process of continual becoming. Removed from the specter of human disasters, he feels that he is freed from imprisonment; far from feeling isolated, he feels that when he and Jim are alone on the river they have substituted the cycle of natural rebirth for the sequence of human decay. Out on the river Huck in effect abandons human time.

Thus if the sensitive Twain narrator feels estranged from his society, he also discovers a means of escape from his loneliness. Images of childhood, of nature (especially associated with water), or of women predominate in these interludes, both for the narrators we have seen and for many of Twain's other characters. These images play similar roles in many of Twain's travel narratives, essays, speeches, and private papers. By studying the contexts in which they appear we will be able to better understand their function as centers of consciousness, as symbols that provide Twain, as well as his characters, with an alternative to his increasingly pessimistic vision of the human condition.

Part II
The Imagery of Contentment

5

Water and Space: The Imagery of Release

In Mark Twain's imagination, water and space provide a source of release from human restrictions. In his early work Twain's most lyrical passages tend to combine images of water with references to escape, daydreams, or contentment, as if, through the very act of composing those passages, the busy writer could withdraw to an imaginary seascape where he could find relief from his anxieties. Similarly, in his later work, descriptions of journeys through outer space are often couched in ecstatic language, occurring in conjunction with references to escape from the limitations of both the body and the mind. Together, water and space are possibly the most central of Twain's preferred images; he uses them, first, to express his ambivalence about the tensions he perceived between himself and the community and, second, as a means to escape the restrictions of the human condition.

Roughing It, published in 1872 but recording Twain's Comstock and San Francisco years (1861–1866), contains one of his earliest published homages to the sensation of being suspended on still water. In a chapter concerning a sojourn at Lake Tahoe, he remembers his chief occupation as "drifting around in the boat . . . we usually pushed out a hundred yards or so from shore, and then lay down on the thwarts, in the sun, and let the boat drift by the hour whither it would. We seldom talked. It interrupted the Sabbath stillness, and marred the dreams the luxurious rest and indolence brought" (*RI,* p. 544). In Twain's memory, the sensation of drifting on still water separated the companions into their own private dream worlds. In addition, the combination of the drifting boat with the remarkably clear water of Tahoe brought an association with flight: "So empty and airy did all spaces seem below us," he recalls, "and so strong was the sense of floating high aloft in mid-nothingness, that we called these boat excursions 'balloon-voyages' " (*RI*, p. 544). The consciousness recording this moment unites water and sky into a universe in which the subject feels released not only from the responsibilities, or psychological restrictions, of the community, but also from the gravity, or physical restrictions, of the land. And in this "Sabbath stillness," Twain's persona experiences the "luxurious rest" that characterizes the spiritual respite for which nearly all his narrative personae are searching, from de Conte's quest for timeless redemption in his vision of the fairy tree to Huck's quest for timeless comfort in his home on the raft.

It is possible that Twain's association of water and space with freedom from limitations dated from his years on the Mississippi, for Albert Bigelow Paine records that during his night watches Twain contemplated the reflection of the night sky in the water and that it induced a state of profound meditation on metaphysical themes.[1] Perhaps the young Sam Clemens did reflect on cosmic questions under the influence of water and sky; perhaps the elderly Mark Twain only remembered it that way. The buoyancy attendant on floating and the effects of flight are similar: both induce an illusion of freedom from gravity, and it is not unlikely that at night the young pilot may have felt his boat gliding in an ethereal realm that fused airy heaven and aqueous earth. Certainly the elderly Twain substituted images of space for images of water when he wanted to portray a character who was not bound by the human condition: in "No. 44, The Mysterious Stranger," for instance, the dreamself claims his special province to be "the Constellations and the Milky Way." *Roughing It* already indicates a profound sense of cosmic reverie in a location that seems to unite water and sky; a notebook entry of 1902 shows that for Twain the association was a lasting one. When the yacht on which he was traveling anchored off the coast of the Bahamas, Twain, keeper of the ship's log, noted: "Arrived at Nassau, 7am. Anchored in a

1. Albert Bigelow Paine, *Mark Twain: A Biography*, p. 154.

long narrow harbor like a lake. White coral bottom, & crystal clear water: in 5 fathoms the ship seemed to float in the air."[2]

This chapter examines the function that the twin images of water and space play in Mark Twain's imagination. Proceeding roughly in chronological order, it first looks at the primacy of water images in Twain's early works (from 1866 to about 1886) and at the manner in which they simultaneously illustrate his sense of alienation from the community and provide images of psychological transcendence that allow him to escape the loneliness that alienation engenders.[3] Ultimately, Twain associates escape from the community with escape from temporality, and, as we saw in "No. 44, The Mysterious Stranger," for Mark Twain temporality was the framework for the irreversible chain of human misery that defined the human condition. When he associates water with escape from the community, he lays the foundation for his eventual association of freedom from the human condition with escape from temporality.

Although he never completely abandons references to water as symbols of escape from human time, images of outer space gain primacy in Twain's middle to late period (about 1886 to 1909); they, too, illustrate his response to his conviction that human history represented a prison from which no act of free will could liberate him. These later images, however, function less as means of psychological transcendence than as philosophical resolutions to the problem that he by then had recognized and was attempting to confront in a rational manner. Furthermore, although both his images of water and his images of space convey a self that conceives of itself as inherently opposed to an Other, as the images shift there is a corresponding shift in the concept to which the Other refers. Despite this change of referents, however, the images function almost

2. Unpublished Notebook, "Log of the Kanawha, Mark Twain: Official Logger," p. 2. The Mark Twain Papers, Bancroft Library, University of California, Berkeley, hereafter cited as MTP.

3. According to Gaston Bachelard, reveries before still waters induce a psychic state in which the world no longer seems to stand in opposition to the subjective consciousness. In such reveries the subject is united to the cosmos and freed from the restrictions that the Other always imposes. From this chapter on, my study is indebted to Bachelard's discussion of "cosmic reverie," the state of solitude that reveals the subject's, or dreamer's, soul and in which the poetic image "bears witness to a soul which is discovering its world, the world where it

identically; both illustrate the author's wish to destroy temporal horizons and both are presented in language so lyrical as to approach the ecstatic. As we shall see, both represent locations where Mark Twain imagined an alienated consciousness could live atemporally and, in escaping the strictures of human time, also escape the tragedy of the human condition.

Like his assessments of human nature, Mark Twain's images of water exhibit the ambivalence that appears to be fundamental to his nature. One peculiarity about his water images is that he uses identical metaphors in apparently opposite ways: both to invite and to reject other people. In 1868, in the course of persuading Olivia Langdon, his future wife, that only she could provide him with a home to replace the one he had lost, Twain had presented himself as "a waif, floating at random upon the sea of life,"[4] and his subsequent letters to Livy abound with similar tropes. Even though they were stock metaphors in nineteenth-century rhetoric, in Twain's writings images of lost vessels appear too often, in too fervent a context, to be dismissed as mere clichés. Time and again he employs phrases that indicate that he took the metaphor for his own and saw himself as a drifting vessel; time and again he suggests that the vessel is searching for a port. A clue to this particular manipulation of water images comes in the last section of "About All Kinds of Ships" (1892), in a narrative segment in which Twain satirizes his first ocean voyage. Here he discusses just how often sea images had appeared in sentimental songs of his childhood. "Everyone on a farm lived chiefly amid the dangers of the deep, in those days, in fancy," he remembers, and clearly the familiarity of lyrics like "O Pilot, 'tis a fearful Night," and "A life on the ocean wave / And a home on the rolling deep" influenced his concepts as well as his vocabulary ("AKS," p. 308).

In the last segment of this article, however, Twain also casts himself in a double role: he is both the narrator who recalls being a member of a group of self-righteous young people and a

would like to live and where it deserves to live" *(The Poetics of Reverie: Childhood, Language, and the Cosmos,* pp. 14–15).

4. *Mark Twain's Collected Letters,* vol. 1, 1853–1869, edited by Lin Salamo, #258. Hereafter abbreviated as *CL,* 1.

"liar" whom the young people tried to reform but who, being incorrigible, was finally "left to himself," a "forsaken figure, leaning forlorn against the taffrail," shut out from the group who sang—endlessly and mindlessly—"Homeward Bound" despite the fact that the boat was becalmed ("AKS," p. 311). We know that the liar is Twain, first, because when the narrator (who has hitherto been trustworthy) describes him he suddenly lapses into the kind of goody-goody rhetoric that signals Mark Twain's rejection of the narrow values of the speaker, and, second, because the story is abruptly closed by a patent lie directly after the narrator has piously recalled his own efforts to redeem the incorrigible one for the community. This doubling of the accepted and the rejected self is typical of the dual purposes to which Twain puts images associated with water throughout his writing: like the tension he indicates between the untrustworthy first-person narrator and the incorrigible alien on a boat going nowhere, Twain uses boat and water references to express his ambivalence about being accepted or rejected by the community. Standing behind all his laments about being a waif on the seas of life is the suggestion that that was precisely the situation in which he experienced the most pleasure.

An example of the way he manipulates his audience when he uses his "lost ship" metaphor occurs as late as 1908, in a speech delivered to an enthusiastic audience in Liverpool just after he was awarded his honorary degree from Oxford University. This image echoes those in Twain's courtship letters, even though here the analogy he is building stresses, through the contrast of two kinds of merchant vessels, the pride he takes in his listeners' homage. At the end of the speech he tells them that their outpouring of enthusiasm has transformed him from a "homely little coasting sloop" into "a stately Indiaman, plowing the great seas under a cloud of canvas and laden with the kindest words that have ever been vouchsafed to any wandering alien in this world, I think."[5] This speech, as Hamlin Hill rightly observes, is a rhetorical tour de force; it is particularly fascinating

5. Hamlin Hill, *Mark Twain: God's Fool*, pp. 176–77.

for the manner in which Twain manipulates his images. Not only does he cast himself in the role of a boat—a watergoing vessel, whether humble or stately—but he also manages to slip in a reference to himself as a homeless alien who has been given respite from his loneliness through the warmth of his audience's approval. As in his letter to Livy, the image of himself as a drifting vessel is used here to convince his listeners that only by an outpouring of love could he be redeemed for the community. When, forty years earlier, he had told Livy, a pious Christian anxious about the state of her lover's soul, that through her devotion he had become "freighted with a good purpose, and blessed with a fair wind, a chart to follow [and] a port to reach,"[6] he was deliberately manipulating the familiar metaphor to convince her that loving him was part of her mission on earth. So, too, could he assure his listeners that their enthusiasm guided him to a safe haven among them.

But these public, persuasive uses of a common trope are best seen as casting light on Twain's private response to being cast away from the shores of respectable society. As his double role in "About All Kinds of Ships" suggests, water images provided him with a double-edged metaphor for demonstrating his ambivalence about being acceptable to the community. He publicly portrays himself as a drifting vessel in order to persuade people to love him, but he privately (and less self-consciously) uses similar images to perform the opposite function: to provide himself with private symbols of escape from the same respectable people from whom he publicly strives to exact affection. He closes his seventieth-birthday speech, delivered at a large banquet honoring him at Delmonico's in 1905, by wishing his listeners well and hoping that "when you in your turn shall arrive at pier No. 70 you may step aboard your waiting ship with a reconciled spirit, and lay your course toward the sinking sun with a contented heart."[7] Here he implies that old age is a welcome "casting off" from shores to which the younger spirit needed reconciling. Both his birthday and his Liverpool speeches are only samples from possibly thousands of refer-

---

6. *CL*, 1, #258.
7. Mark Twain, *Speeches* (New York: Harper and Brothers, 1923), 24: 262.

ences to himself as a boat. Although he implies that the boat is lost when he wants to evoke a response from an audience, generally he uses the image to express his joy at the prospect of getting away from other people.

References to water always figure prominently in Mark Twain's writing. In part, this is due to his propensity to borrow a popular image and make it serve his peculiar design, but it is also due to the fact that bodies of water were literally central to his life. He grew up on the Mississippi, and his years piloting a steamboat were only a prelude to numerous sea journeys and to residence in houses within easy reach of oceans and rivers.[8] Continual exposure to any geographical element is likely to be reflected in an artist's work, but the centrality of water images in Twain's writing makes them more than simply mirrors of his physical environment. We know that in *Adventures of Huckleberry Finn* Twain associates the shore with the community and the river with escape from it, but it is important to note that in the late 1870s this particular schema was only the most clearly formulated manifestation of an association that he had long held. In *Roughing It* he already indicates that he associated drifting with reverie; earlier references to periods spent adrift on bodies of water suggest that even then he associated them with release from communal demands. In 1866, on his return from his visit to the Sandwich Islands sponsored by the *Sacramento Union*, he spent twenty-five days becalmed on the ship *Smyrniote*, an experience that provided the material for the story of the liar in "All Kinds of Ships" thirty years later. Although his notebook entries during the journey indicate that he was exasperated by the delay, letters written at the same time indicate that he enjoyed it: "I suppose, from present appearances—light winds & calms—that we shall be two or three weeks at sea,

---

8. Of course, prior to the advent of the railroad, most towns tended to be situated near a river, a lake, or the ocean. The major towns and their adjacent bodies of water in which Clemens lived were as follows: Hannibal, the Mississippi River; San Francisco, the Pacific Ocean; Hartford, the Connecticut River; Elmira, the Chemung River; Heidelberg, the Neckar River; Berlin, the Spree and the Havel rivers; Florence, the Arno River; Munich, the Isar River; London, the Thames River; Vienna, the Danube River; Bermuda, the Atlantic Ocean; New

yet—and I hope so—I am in no hurry to go back to work."[9] And
the notebook entry he made just after landing in San Francisco
reveals an unexpectedly violent reaction to his return: "Aug.
13—San Francisco—Home again. No—*not* home again—in
prison again—so cramped, and so weary with toil and care and
business anxiety. God help me, I wish I were at sea again!"[10]
Clearly, Twain saw the trip, including the days spent becalmed,
as a period of rest away from the "cramped" life on shore. One of
the first results of the calm was that he made more notebook
entries than usual. While none of them is of special significance
in itself, together they show that the journey gave the busy
young writer a chance to record his impressions of the Islands
and to mull over their potential for literary development.

Not all of Twain's periods at sea were spent becalmed, but his
response to later sea journeys, or to any water journey where he
was not actively piloting the ship, tended to echo the contentment he felt on the *Smyrniote* trip. In 1868 he wrote to Mrs.
Fairbanks, the "foster mother" whom he had met on the
Quaker City excursion to the Holy Land, "I am *so* glad of an
excuse to go to sea again, even for three weeks,"[11] and even
when he was on a journey that proceeded without delays, the
very experience of being on water evoked echoes of his contentment at being becalmed. For instance, in *A Tramp Abroad*
(1880) he contrasts a rafting trip down the Neckar River to all
modes of transportation on land, concluding that only water
journeys provide the necessary avenue to repose, for "the motion of the raft is the needful motion. It is gentle and gliding and
smooth and noiseless, it calms down all feverish activities, it
soothes to sleep all nervous hurry and impatience. Under its
restful influence all the troubles and vexations and sorrows that
harass the mind vanish away, and existence becomes a dream, a
charm, a deep and tranquil ecstacy" (*TA*, p. 104). His journey not
only takes him away from the frustrations of the land, it also

---

York City, the Hudson and East rivers and the Atlantic Ocean; Stormfield, the
Saugatuck River.

9. *CL*, 1, #128.

10. *Mark Twain's Notebooks and Journals*, vol. 1, 1855–1873, edited by
Frederick Anderson, Michael B. Frank, and Kenneth Sanderson. Hereafter
abbreviated as *N&J*, 1.

11. *CL*, 1, #197.

permits him to participate in the plenum of nature, to "see the sun create the new morning." Like Huck, out on the river Twain is reminded of the cycle of natural rebirth, and that reminder, coupled with the motion of the raft, brings him his "deep and tranquil ecstasy."

As Mark Twain developed the rhetorical power of his water images he also developed the antithesis, or series of antitheses, that provides the framework for his use of water images as symbols of escape from human time. In *Life on the Mississippi* (1882), in a passage ostensibly lamenting the decline of business on the river, he notes,

> the day goes, the night comes, and again the day—and still the same, night after night and day after day after day—majestic, unchanging sameness of serenity, repose, tranquility, lethargy, vacancy—symbol of eternity, realization of the heaven pictured by priest and prophet. (*LM*, p. 166)

As we shall see, "serenity, repose, tranquility, lethargy, vacancy" become verbal trail markers on Mark Twain's private path to cosmic reverie. Carefully pacing his phrases, and never moving beyond the present tense, he constructs this passage so that repose becomes equated with eternity, "the heaven pictured by priest and prophet." Unlike the heaven in *Captain Stormfield's Visit to Heaven*, which satirizes the idea of the afterlife held by petty townspeople who see it as being as sociable—even as frenetic—as their temporal life, here Mark Twain pictures heaven as a vast vacancy, where the subject's consciousness moves through a landscape so still as to imply stasis. Drifting past stretches of Mississippi shore that are devoid of visible signs of habitation induces such a state of stasis; a landscape that does not change suggests that the perceiver is not going anywhere. The sensation is nonteleological, anticipating the immutability of eternity.

By 1897, Mark Twain understood that the suggestion of stasis constituted the appeal of the sea voyage for him. In a brief episode in *Following the Equator*, recording the long, slow passage between Ceylon and Mauritius, he claims,

> I do not know how a day could be more reposeful: no motion; a level

blue sea; nothing in sight from horizon to horizon; the speed of the ship furnishes a cooling breeze; there is no mail to read and answer; no newspapers to excite you; no telegrams to fret you or fright you—the world is far, far away; it has ceased to exist for you— seemed a fading dream, along in the first days; has dissolved to an unreality now; it is gone from your mind with its businesses and ambitions, its prosperities and disasters, its exultations and despairs, its joys and griefs and cares and worries. They are no concern of yours any more; they have gone out of your life; they are a storm which has passed and left a deep calm behind. (*FE*, p. 1032)

References to repose occur frequently in such passages; here they are explicitly related to escape from the frenetic social life the public man led on shore. As in the passage from *Life on the Mississippi*, here the illusion of timelessness is signaled by Twain's almost constant use of the present tense, which fixes the moment by making it impossible to show time passing. Only two conditional clauses move beyond the magic moment, and those to a hypothetical realm that would perpetuate it. "I myself am wholly indifferent as to when we are going to 'get in,' " Twain continues. "If I had my way we should never get in at all. This sort of sea life is charged with an indestructible charm. There is no weariness, no fatigue, no worry, no responsibility, no work, no depression of spirits." And again, echoing the passage from *Life on the Mississippi*, "There is nothing like this serenity, this comfort, this peace, this deep contentment, to be found anywhere on land. If I had my way I would sail on for ever and never go to live on the solid ground again" (*FE*, p. 1032).

The simple lyricism of this passage suggests the intensity with which Twain valued such periods. *Following the Equator* is his record of the lecture tour he undertook to recoup the money he had lost on the Paige typesetter and other investments; between the end of the trip and the composition of the book his daughter Susy died and his close family relationships began to dissolve, a process that Hamlin Hill has carefully documented in *Mark Twain: God's Fool*. As Charles Neider comments in his introduction to the travel narratives, it is miraculous that the book was written at all; Twain partly attributed its completion to the fact that writing every day allowed him to forget his troubles.[12]   But the fact that during a period of genuine crisis he saw water journeys, especially sea journeys, as escapes from tension emphasizes the power the image had for him. Being suspended at sea is like being suspended in time; it creates the illusion that the flow of history can be halted and an idyllic interlude can be expanded to an eternal moment. By wishing never to arrive at the shore, where the flow of history is not only irreversible but merciless, Twain shows just how deeply he treasured the idea that time might be stopped and the indeterminacy of the journey extended.

Mark Twain was certainly not the first writer to metaphorically associate experiences of being on water with timelessness; however, in this context Maurice Merleau-Ponty's discussion of the metaphor is helpful in understanding the specific terms of Twain's association. In *Phenomenology of Perception*, Merleau-Ponty discusses the confusion that has resulted from the tradition, effective at least since Heraclitus, to speak of time metaphorically as a river. This metaphor, Merleau-Ponty claims, presupposes a viewer and ignores the fact that the river *as* a river does not possess a sense of its relationship to the shore, that is, it does not observe itself flowing. Rather, like the rest of the natural world, it exists without spatial or temporal reference to anything else. Time is not introduced into the natural world until a viewer is placed in relation to it. In the world itself, *for* itself, time collapses; the river *is* wherever it is, it is not "past" upstream and "future" downstream. Rather, "the objective world is too much of a plenum for there to be time."[13]   Consequently, time exists only for the viewer on the shore who watches the river roll past, or for the viewer in a boat who watches the shores as they seem to pass by. Time does *not* exist if there is nothing to measure it by; and hence in his moments of drifting on still waters, freed, at least imaginatively, from hori-

12. Charles Neider, ed., *The Complete Travel Books of Mark Twain*, 1:xxvi. In a letter to Twichell on 19 January 1897, Twain claimed, "I am working, but it is for the sake of the work—the 'surcease of sorrow' that is found there. I work all the days, and trouble vanishes away when I use that magic." This letter is discussed further in the last chapter. Noted in Bernard DeVoto, "The Symbols of Despair," in *Mark Twain at Work*, p. 143.

13. Maurice Merleau-Ponty, *Phenomenology of Perception*, p. 412.

zons, Mark Twain levels time by abolishing past and future. He exists, temporarily, in an eternal present. That is why Huck Finn, echoing Mark Twain when the latter returned from his first sea voyage, finds that the shore, not the boat, feels "cramped." How can one feel cramped in eternity?

It is precisely this sense of timelessness and plenitude in the natural world that stands behind the lyricism of the river scenes in Twain's Mississippi valley pieces. Certainly Huckleberry Finn communes with nature rather than with other people; even his intimacy with Jim is part of his escape into the natural world, for much of Mark Twain's portrayal of Jim is ruled by the stereotype that sees the black as spiritually closer to nature than the abstract, desensitized white. In their magic otherworld, Huck's alienation from the community becomes his means to experience brief moments outside of human time. For within the community time is *kept*; its passage is marked by the observance of a series of rituals: "You had to wash, and eat on a plate, and comb up, and go to bed and get up regular, and be forever bothering over a book, and have old Miss Watson pecking at you all the time," Huck recalls, in a series of polysyndetic conjuncts that he uses to imply how the community's temporal regulations accumulate to restrict his every move (*HF*, p. 22).

On the river, however, such regulations do not exist; consequently, neither does Huck's sense of time. There, "days and nights swum by, they slid along so quiet and smooth and lovely" (*HF*, p. 99). In fact, in his very best moments on the river Huck perceives all time as one time and all events as one event. In the eternal moment he creates through his perception of the oneness of time he is not an observer playing a part, as he is whenever he participates in community events; rather, he is a passive—and infinitely contented—participant in an experience that is, ultimately, the transcendence of time.

In Merleau-Ponty's terms, Huck's essential passivity enables him, more than any other observer in Mark Twain's work, to perceive the self-containing circle of plenitude. When Huck conveys the unity of the natural world to us he conveys it with a sense of its integrity. Because he speaks a nonstandard dialect, Huck can convey the unity of natural time by way of a grammatical confusion that merges past and present and implies the future. The famous passage describing dawn on the river rests on this confusion. First, Huck sees

> a pale place in the sky; then more paleness, spreading around; then the river softened up, away off, and warn't black any more, but gray; you could see little dark spots drifting along, ever so far away —trading scows, and such things; and long black streaks—rafts; sometimes you could hear a sweep screaking; or jumbled up voices, it was so still, and sounds come so far; and by-and-by you could see a streak on the water which you know by the look of the streak that there's a snag there in a swift current which breaks on it and makes that streak look that way; and you see the mist curl up off of the water, and the east reddens up. (*HF*, p. 100)

Here Huck moves from a present to a past tense, and from there to an imperfect past before returning to the present. In the process he conveys all sunrises in his portrait of this particular one, and by speaking in the second person instead of the first he implies a unity with other perceivers. In the image of a dawn on the river that contains all dawns on all rivers he thus demonstrates a sense of fulfillment that he can achieve in no other situation, for in his suggestion that this dawn represents all dawns, he also suggests that he represents all perceivers of dawns in an eternity in which perceiver and perceived are one. The sense of deep contentment conveyed by Twain's descriptions of his hours drifting in the stillness of Lake Tahoe, or of being becalmed on the Pacific, or of his days on the South Seas suspended between Ceylon and Mauritius is also conveyed by Huck's description of his life on the raft.[14] "There ain't no home like a raft," Huck claims when he escapes the bloody tragedy at

14. One of the most recent critics to work with this passage is George C. Carrington, Jr., who, in *The Dramatic Unity of Huckleberry Finn*, a structuralist analysis, remarks that in his reverie "Huck has his moment of epiphany, his union with nature and with the moral world; but that moment can only be a moment, one situation in a succession of situations" (p. 147). Carrington's study shows that Twain was interested in "situational man," the character who creates his own dramas and whose language reflects "situational choices"— tribal referents reflecting Carrington's thesis that *Huckleberry Finn* is about the human need for drama. While it is true that during his ecstatic moments "Huck has had a glimpse of better things . . . but in a situational world the glimpse is only momentary" (p. 147), his moments of reverie cannot be dismissed quite so summarily. As all glimpses are, this glimpse may be only momentary, but the

the Grangerford's. "Home" is where the soul is at rest, and floating in a timeless sphere becomes "Home" to Twain and to the characters who represent that aspect of his consciousness.

While Twain's images of water reveal an effort to transcend human time through the creation of an eternal present, his images of outer space reveal an effort to overcome the tyranny of chronology through philosophical meditation. Between the plenum of nature in which Huck sheds his loneliness and reveals his soul, and the vastness of outer space in which August discovers his solipsistic omnipotence, Twain's central metaphor for escape from human time shifted from earth to heaven. Like his water metaphors, Twain's spatial metaphors explore the relationship between self and other, but the other with whom he is concerned here is his other self, not other people. At the same time that he was venting his frustrations about the inadequacies of his nation's—and other nations'—moral progress through a series of furious essays ("To the Person Sitting in Darkness," "The United States of Lyncherdom," and "King Leopold's Soliloquy" are three of the best-known examples), he was working out a series of spatial images that show that he had transformed his search for a resolution to his own alienation from an external to an internal one. He developed these images both in his notebook entries and in his unfinished fiction; their significance, like the significance of his water images, was clarified only after he had begun using them, when it became evident that the cosmos to which he ultimately was referring was of the ideal rather than the empirical universe. In his work spatial images tend to replace water images as metaphors for freedom from human limitations, but in late life he decided that such freedom was to be sought not in the plenum, the empirical world, but in interior space, the space that, according to Georges Poulet, "separates me from, or draws me closer to, that which I am able to think."[15]

One of the first indications that Twain saw his mind as a mirror of the cosmos appears, appropriately, in his reflections

moment is charged with the emotional quality the idea of eternity held for Mark Twain.

15. Georges Poulet, *The Interior Distance*, preface.

about his intellectual experiences. As Alan Gribben has recently shown,[16] Twain's interest in Robert Browning's poetry was in large part stimulated by the fact that the poet's monologues were admirably suited to Twain's particular style of public reading. He worked hard to understand the poet's meanings, and on 23 February 1887 he noted on the flyleaf of his much-annotated copy of *Dramatis Personae*, "One's glimpses and confusions, as one reads Browning, remind me of looking through a telescope. . . . You toil across dark spaces which are (to *your* lens) empty; but every now and then a splendor of stars and suns bursts upon you and fills the whole field with flame."[17] That the process of understanding should be explained by use of such extraterrestrial imagery indicates a sensibility that does not conceive of itself in limited, human terms but at the same time seeks intimate contact with others. The verb *toil* echoes Christian symbolism of the soul's journey toward God through a world of sorrows; here the toilsome journey is through the void toward contact with another mind, a contact signaled by a burst of light. In this notation the topography of the universe clearly stands for the topography of Twain's own mind, indicating that he envisioned his searching consciousness as a single entity roaming in a vast, dark space.

Ten years later Twain was deep in mourning for Susy, his oldest child, who had died of meningitis at the age of twenty-three. It is clear from photographs that Susy looked like her father, and he seems to have felt that of the three girls, she was most like him. Several of his notebook entries in the year following her death compare her proficiencies—and deficiencies—to his own. He also writes about her intellectual powers, using words that, like his Browning notation, suggest that he envisioned the act of comprehension as like a splash of brilliant light upon a dark void. In a eulogistic passage that is partly crossed out and revised (although it was never published), Twain chooses words like *depth*, *scope*, and *stretch* to characterize Susy's "intellectual vision" and compares her ability to understand literature and articulate its meaning to "a single flash" of her mind upon a "dark page."[18]

16. Alan Gribben, " 'A Splendor of Stars and Sun': Twain as a Reader of Browning's Poems."

17. Paine, *Mark Twain's Biography*, p. 847.

18. Unpublished Notebook, 30, II (1 June 1896–16 July 1896), p. 57. MTP.

It is interesting that Twain uses images similar to ones he uses to describe his own mind in order to convey the intellectual prowess of his favorite child. It not only indicates how much he felt her to resemble him, it also sheds extra light on his comprehension of his mental geography. Here too the act of comprehension is explained through images that indicate that he pictured his interior space as a reflection of the universe. But conveying understanding was only the beginning of his use of extraterrestrial images. Twain's later writings suggest that he may have concluded that the mind—specifically, his own—was the single entity capable of escaping temporality; significantly, he conveys his ideas through spatial images.

Like many of his contemporaries, Mark Twain had long been interested in mental phenomena. Not only did he write articles about mental telepathy, his notebook entries also contain numerous references to conversations about the relationship between dreams and reality. In 1884, entries indicate that he, William Dean Howells, and Thomas Bailey Aldrich were conducting an extended debate about dreams, about their duration in concrete time, their power to predict events, their pictorial as opposed to their verbal qualities, and their significance as symbols.[19] Nor was the subject confined to Howells and Aldrich among Twain's circle; in January of that year Henry C. Robinson, a Hartford lawyer, read a paper on dreams before the Monday Evening Club, an informal male organization in which Twain was an active member. In 1897 Twain made extensive notes on the relationship of consciousness to dreams, and for years he had been logging incidents of mental telepathy, from speculations concerning simultaneous inventions to conversations between family members where one guessed the other's next words.[20] In his article "Mental Telegraphy" he says that he began collecting anecdotes about telepathic coincidences in 1875, and in that essay, which he claims to have begun while writing *A Tramp Abroad*, he documents his own telepathic experiences.[21]

---

19. *Mark Twain's Notebooks and Journals*, vol. 3, 1883–1891, edited by Robert Pack Browning, Michael B. Frank, and Lin Salamo, p. 462. Hereafter cited as *N&J*, 3.
20. Ibid., pp. 20, 488.
21. Mark Twain, "Mental Telegraphy," in *In Defense of Harriet Shelley* (New York: Harper and Brothers, 1925).

The results of these speculations are revealed privately in Twain's letters and journals as well as fictively in works like "No. 44, The Mysterious Stranger." When he notes in his journal that his "spiritualized self" is "merely my ordinary body and mind freed from clogging flesh and become a spiritualized body and mind,"[22] he indicates that he sensed a creative other shadowing his familiar self, an other not subject to the "gravitational" forces that bind human beings to the earth. The dream experience was crucial to his exploration of that other because he felt that in dreams his creative consciousness was released from the strictures of time and space. Consequently, examining dreams became a major preoccupation, one most clearly exhibited in what may loosely be called his nightmare manuscripts, a series of novels that were mostly unfinished and unpublished in his lifetime.[23] In them Twain explores the connections between dreams and reality, moving from one level of psychic reality to another and altering temporal relationships as his characters change from their dreaming to their waking lives. These works show that the concept of worlds within worlds became Twain's basic schema to describe the relationship between self and other. In his nightmare manuscripts his protagonists tend to be trapped in terrible circumstances, either within a nightmare from which they cannot awake or within a microscopic world from which they cannot escape. First-person narrators all, the protagonists of these tales universally see themselves as alien to their surroundings, and they express their longings to be "free" in terms that as often refer to outer space as to some previous earthly existence.

One of the longest and loveliest of his references to outer space occurs in the manuscript fragment "3,000 Years Among the Microbes," written in 1905. In a radical extension of Twain's tendency to denigrate the body, here the protagonist (who has been turned into a microbe) is trapped inside the body of a bum, who, diseased and corrupted, is filled with minute beings whose lives are conducted without their being conscious that there exists any other world but "Henryland," the body of

22. Albert Bigelow Paine, ed., *Mark Twain's Notebook*, pp. 348–52.
23. Recently edited by John S. Tuckey under the title *Mark Twain's Which*

the host. Lecturing his microbe friends on his old, lost home, the protagonist tells them,

> There that little world—so unimaginably vast, compared with yours!—paddles about in a shoreless solitude of space; and where are those millions of others? Lost! —vanished! invisible, when the great sun rides in the sky; but at night—oh, there they are! colossal black hulks, lumbering by? No! —turned to mere glinting sparks by distance! —a distance not conceivable by such as you! The vault is strewn thick with them, the vault is alive with them, trembles with them, quivers with them! And through their midst rises a broad belt of their like, uncountable for number—rises and flows up into the sky, from the one horizon, and pours across and goes flooding down to the other—a stupendous arch, made all of glittering vast suns diminished to twinkling points by the awful distance—and where is that colossal planet of mine? It's *in* that Belt—somewhere, God knows where! It wanders there somewhere in that immeasurable ocean of twinkling fires, and takes up no more room and gets no more notice than would a firefly that was adrift in the deeps of the opal skies that bend over imperial Henryland! ("3,000 Years," pp. 486–87)

The concept of relative spatiality indicated here has its counterpart in Twain's concept of relative temporality. Both had their roots in Twain's invectives against the human condition; as early as 1884 he was noting, "I think we are only the microscopic trichina concealed in the blood of some vast creature's veins, and that it is that vast creature God concerns himself about, and not us."[24] As he transformed these naive ideas into fiction, however, he began to explore the far more interesting questions that they raised, especially those concerning perception and the "double-vision" of a consciousness that knows that there are worlds beyond the one in which it finds itself. These immediately involved him in questions of relative time and space. The stories concerning a human consciousness exploring a microscopic world are closely related to those concerning a waking consciousness exploring a dream world, first, because in both the protagonist knows that he is trapped among beings who do not themselves know that there exist worlds beyond

Was the Dream? and other Symbolic Writings of the Later Years. I often refer to the works in this volume as the "nightmare manuscripts."

24. *N&J*, 3, p. 56.

their own and, second, because the protagonist necessarily is aware of two levels of temporality: his own and that of the alien world around him.

In "3,000 Years," for instance, the narrator perceives time both from a microbe's and from a human's points of view: "my human measurements of time and my human span of life remained to me, right alongside of my full appreciation of the germ-measurements of time and the germ span of life" ("3,000 Years," p. 435). In other words his human consciousness perceives that his lifespan is three thousand times longer than that of his microbe companions: during the first three weeks of his transformation he has seen "billions of [microbe] friends . . . pass from this fleeting life to return no more!" ("3,000 Years," p. 437). As in the biblical adage that one thousand years are as an eyeblink to the Lord, here Twain implies that time and space are relative to the magnitude of the mind measuring them. Part of his philosophical reasoning resulted in his seeing existence as a series of Chinese boxes, each containing a universe of beings having no conception that they are merely "microbes" in the body of a far larger being. Since time and space are relative to the size of the universe in which they are measured, it is not inconceivable that a being might exist who is not bound by any particular universe and therefore by any particular time and space. For that transcendent being, "home" would lie beyond all conceivable worlds. When the protagonist of "3,000 Years" documents his experiences, he must translate their duration into "microbe time," not a difficult task, he claims, for "since ever so long ago, microbe time has been *real* to me, and human time a dream" ("3,000 Years," p. 449). His meditations on this phenomenon lead him to the suspicion, based on his own experiences, that "man is himself a microbe, and his globe a blood-corpuscle drifting with its shining brethren of the Milky-Way down a vein of the Master and Maker of all things. Whose body, mayhap—glimpsed partwise from earth by night, and receding and lost to view in the measureless remotenesses of space—is what men name the Universe" ("3,000 Years," p. 454).

It may be useful in this context to look briefly again at the philosophy of Merleau-Ponty, here not in direct reference to temporality but in relation to the cogito. In examining

Descartes's second meditation, Merleau-Ponty claims that if we follow Descartes's reasoning from things to thought about things, we can take one of two courses, to see experience, that is, the "I," as the grand collector of psychological events—in which case we can be no more certain that the collector exists than we are that the events do—or to recognize the "I" as anterior to events, as "a field and a system of thoughts . . . subject neither to time nor to any other limitations." From this point of view, consciousness and existence are recognizable as one, as "a spiritual act which grasps at a distance and compresses into itself everything at which it aims . . . an 'I think' which is, by itself, and without any adjunct, an 'I am.' "[25]

For Merleau-Ponty, the Cartesian doctrine of the cogito leads inevitably to the claim that mind is timeless because as the entity anterior to all events, it becomes that capacity for events that is eternity. Although Merleau-Ponty—himself not a philosophical idealist—carefully analyzes and qualifies this assertion, as it stands it is a tool we can use to look at Twain's philosophy of mind, which, even though it exhibits his lack of familiarity with formal philosophy, is probing and experiential. Clearly one of the reasons Twain was so interested in dreams was that they seemed to collapse time and space; he understood that the subjective consciousness experienced a radical disjunction between what it seemed possible to accomplish in sleeping time and what seemed possible in waking time. While he explored the possibility of layered temporalities in works like "3,000 Years," he explored the possibility of alternate temporalities in works like "Which Was It?" (also one of the science fiction, or nightmare, manuscripts). In these the protagonists (often voluntarily) enter a dream world for an experiment, only to find that the dream has become the reality. If they are lucky enough to escape the dream (a circumstance often dependent on whether or not the manuscript was completed), they find that the days or months or years of their dream life have been compressed into no more than minutes of their "real" one. In "The Great Dark," Mark Twain manages to combine *all* of his strategies for temporal exploration: the protagonist embarks on his investigation into the life of the other through the agency of

25. Merleau-Ponty, *Phenomenology of Perception*, p. 372.

the "Superintendent of Dreams," but the dream takes place on a boat that is on a vast, landless sea that is actually a drop of water seen through a microscope. As the only person on board who has faith in the memory of his previous life, the protagonist tries to convince his wife that it, and not ship life, is the real one, but faced with her disbelief—and her tears—he stops fighting and resorts to recording his doubts on paper. "Are we real creatures in a real world," he suddenly wonders, "and have we been feeding on dreams in an imaginary one since nobody knows when—or how *is* it?" ("GD," p. 130). Ultimately, he cannot distinguish which reality is *the* reality, and when the manuscript stops none of us is certain which was the dream.

Twain's most extended discussion of the question of alternate realities appears first in his notebooks and then in "No. 44, The Mysterious Stranger." In his notebook he decides that he shares his body with another consciousness, a doppelgänger he calls his spiritualized-self. Significantly, he imagines the life of that other in spatial terms. Not only is the spiritualized self "freed from clogging flesh and become a spiritualized body and mind," it is also unrestricted by time and distance: "Waking, I move slowly; but in my dreams my unhampered spiritualized body flies to the ends of the earth in a millionth of a second."[26] In an entry much cut by Albert Bigelow Paine when he edited the notebooks, Twain, after examining cases he considers to exhibit the "Jekyll and Hyde theory" of split personality (wherein the two personalities could be interchanged at will) as well as others in which the schizophrenic personalities apparently had no consciousness of each other's existence, decides, first, that the two personalities in a man (the dream-self and the waking-self) are utterly separate and cannot be influenced by each other and, second, that the dream-self is active while the waking-self is asleep. However, Twain also concludes that "we have a *spiritualized self* which can *detach itself* and go wandering off upon affairs of its own," and this self, unlike his dream-self, he *does* know, because "we have a common *memory:* when I wake, mornings, I remember (pretty clearly) what it (that is, *I*) have been doing, and whither it (that is, I) have been wandering in the

---

26. Unpublished Notebook, notebook number 32, I, p. 4. MTP.

course of what I took to be *unrealities*, and called Dreams, for want of a truthfuller name."[27] This is the self in which Twain is interested, both because it influences his waking-self and because it possesses the power to move about without physical encumbrances. In subsequent writings he tended to confuse his dream-self and his spiritualized-self, and in "No. 44, The Mysterious Stranger" the Stranger, too, has some of the latter's qualities.

As John S. Tuckey has noted, passages like these seem to contradict Twain's assertions, militantly stated in "No. 44, The Mysterious Stranger," "What Is Man?," and other writings, that "a man *originates* nothing in his head, he merely observes exterior things, and *combines* them in his head."[28] This mechanistic—and ultimately pessimistic—conclusion has led most readers to see Twain as a materialist, misanthropically expounding doctrines that he thought heretical but that were actually fairly tired by the time he discovered them. But such conclusions must—like almost all statements of Twain's—be seen in the context of his response to his own experience of the world, and this takes its place within the context both of Twain's rejection of human history and of his search for a way to understand his own creativity. The frustration evident in such conclusions reveals a man who *wanted* to think "new thoughts," to originate, to create. In his notebooks Twain wrote that even though he could not "form a face of any kind by a deliberate effort of the imagination," faces "came to" him when he shut his eyes and let his mind wander.[29] The intense curiosity stimulated by this certainty indicates a man seriously trying to probe the mysteries of consciousness, and the conclusion that man is "moved, directed, COMMANDED, by *exterior* influences—*solely*" ("WM?," p. 5) indicates, if nothing else, that he had meditated very deeply on the subject. His materialistic

27. Ibid.
28. John S. Tuckey, "Mark Twain's Later Dialogue: The 'Me' and the Machine," *American Literature* 41 (January 1970): 532–42. Tuckey also sees Twain's exploration of his spiritualized-self as an attempt to find a basis for belief in survival after death and notes that in "No. 44, MS" Twain is making a conscious effort to find the relationship between the dream mind and other levels of consciousness.
29. Unpublished Notebook, notebook number 30, II, p. 59. MTP.

determinism is part of his conclusion that the entire human organism, mind and body, is only a machine, and a poorly functioning one at that.

But the machine-mind only describes the waking-self, the temporal being whom 44 castigates in "No. 44, The Mysterious Stranger." Explicit in Twain's notebook entries is the conclusion that there is something beyond that waking-self, a consciousness that "sends" him pictures; that can, in cases of mental telepathy, make instantaneous contact with another mind. And it is this other "self" or being that he values because he sees in it the escape from temporality that he seeks. As he describes it, this other is tantamount to the cogito examined by Merleau-Ponty; it exists anterior to the waking-self, and it projects itself toward the objects of its desires without restrictions of time or space. Consequently, it is most aptly described in extraterrestrial imagery.

In "No. 44, The Mysterious Stranger," it is clear that the characteristic Twain found most intriguing was the one that enabled all his "other" characters—spirits and strangers alike —to escape the human condition. For instance, in one of his attempts to make August understand the difference between a free spirit and a human being, No. 44 lectures him about the prison that concrete time creates. "Look here, August: there are really no divisions of time—none at all," he begins.

> The past is always present when I want it—the *real* past, not an image of it; I can summon it, and there it *is*. The same with the future: I can summon it out of the unborn ages, and there it is, before my eyes, alive and real, not a fancy, an image, a creation of the imagination. Ah, these troublesome limitations of yours! —they hamper me. ("No. 44, MS," p. 332)

The being for whom there are no divisions of time escapes "this human life, this earthy life, this weary life," as the dream-self characterizes his period of incarnation. Freed from "this loathsome sack of corruption," as we noted earlier, the "spirits of the air" "do not know time . . . do not know space—we live; and love, and labor, and enjoy, fifty years in an hour . . . we circumnavigate your little globe while you wink; we are not tied within horizons" ("No. 44, MS," p. 370).

Both 44 and August's dream-self are articulating Twain's concept of the mind's potential when it is released from the temporality that mandates causality. Here freedom is found in

> *general space*—that sea of ether which has no shores, and stretches on, and on, and arrives nowhere; which is a waste of black gloom and thick darkness through which you may rush forever at thought-speed, encountering at weary long intervals spirit-cheering archipelagoes of suns which rise sparkling far in front of you, and swiftly grow and swell, and burst into blinding glories of light, apparently measureless in extent, but you plunge through and in a moment they are far behind, a twinkling archipelago again, and in another moment they are blotted out in darkness. ("No. 44, MS," p. 377)

Like the description by the protagonist of "3,000 Years Among the Microbes" of his lost home, and like many of Huck's descriptions of the river, this is an ecstatic vision because it lifts the speaker out of his temporal state into an atemporal one and teaches the speaker's audience (here us, as readers) that their historical lives are not the only possible existences. As in Twain's descriptions of drifting on still waters, the present tense predominates, mating form and content and communicating the dissolution of temporal divisions; as in Huck's description of sunrise on the river, the substitution of the second person for the first includes the reader in the revelation. Unlike Twain's descriptions of being on water, however, this passage emphasizes continual movement. Twain seeks stasis on water because it creates the illusion that there are no horizons; he can celebrate movement through outer space precisely because there there are "no shores." In either situation the consciousness being described is joyously surrounded by spaces that seem infinite.

Most questors who have concluded that the universe contains a great Nothing have been terrified by the revelation; they tend to echo Pascal's moving confession that "the eternal Silence of these infinite spaces frightens me." Mark Twain, however, is fascinated by the silence and loneliness of the infinite. Despite his avowal of mechanistic determinism, through passages like those above he indicates he also suspected that if he could think such thoughts, they must reflect an alternative reality, and that he must have experienced such a reality in an alternative state of existence, that is, through his existence as his spiritualized-self. If his contact with his other happens in interior space (that is, in his mind, through his dreams) and if he can communicate with the other or, even better, *become* the other instead of "waking" to his terrestrial self, he will overcome his human limitations and be free to roam through "shoreless space." In his most desperate hours he tries to convince himself that his other existence is the real one: "When we remember that we are all mad, the mysteries disappear and life stands explained," he noted in 1899, six months after the death of his brother Orion.[30] If, at such times, he could convince himself that temporal life merely reflects the nightmares of a dreamer gone berserk, he could by implication escape in the inverse idea that when the dreamer dreamed "other dreams," all would be better.

In "No. 44, The Mysterious Stranger," as we have seen, Twain's hope for a better world is transformed into an accep-tance of the writer's responsibility for the worlds he has created. The last chapter of this study examines Twain's conception of the writer's function in the creation of new worlds; for now, let us note that he saw the idealized self, for itself, as timeless. Discussing the idealist implications of Descartes's meditation, Merleau-Ponty sees them leading to the conclusion that "eternity, understood as the power to embrace and anticipate temporal developments in a single intention, becomes the very definition of subjectivity,"[31] the subjectivity we encounter in August's discovery that he is the only existent thought. In Mark Twain's other writings images of water and space anticipate the philosophy of creative subjectivity articulated in "No. 44, The Mysterious Stranger": drifting on water, or floating through space, his protagonists lose their sense of physical and spiritual restrictions and experience themselves as free of the strictures of ordinary human life. Through these images Twain develops his concept of his other, *real* self, a creative consciousness liberated from the flesh and at home in a universe where it need not even recognize the concepts of time and space.

30. Ibid., notebook number 32b, II, p. 66. MTP.
31. Merleau-Ponty, *Phenomenology of Perception*, p. 372.

6

Childhood: The Imagery of Unity

Twain's discovery that his childhood in the Mississippi valley was good literary material opened the floodgates of his middle, and best, period of writing; moreover, he developed a new device for exploring the tensions between the individual and his society when he learned how to organize his materials around the child's point of view. In order to evaluate the results of these tensions, however, Twain needed a means of measuring them, a more subtle challenge than he may have at once recognized. Unlike his social novels—especially those set in the Middle Ages—where the protagonist stands in opposition to institutions that are clearly unjust, in his novels about childhood on the Mississippi, Twain had to account for his recognition that his protagonists would have to adopt conventional values if they were to become successful individuals. Within the personal history he was turning into fiction lay the roots of his own contradictions: the desire to be an accepted, even adulated, member of the society and the desire to repudiate its conventions and live as an alienated outlaw. When he wrote about conflicts between children and adults, he had to confront the fact that if he repudiated all the institutions that shaped his protagonists' lives he would be repudiating everything for which he was striving himself. Not a Thoreau, anxious to abandon the life of the town, and never able to formulate openly his own version of Emerson's resolution to ride alternately on the horses of his private and public nature, Mark Twain was not interested in renouncing the house, the wife, the servants, the dinners, the transatlantic journeys, or any of the other hallmarks of his own success. Consequently, in evaluating the tensions of childhood he could not entirely reject the process that had landed him where he was, even though, as his satires of small-town life amply illustrate, he simultaneously perceived most conventional behavior as senseless and hypocritical.

Twain resolved this conflict by representing two kinds of childhood, one justifying the process whereby a child is taught how to become a member of his community, the other justifying the process whereby a child escapes the community's confines. On the one hand, Twain recognizes the necessity of restricting children's freedom and conveys his acceptance of that need through an omniscient narrator who mediates between rebellious boys and their authoritarian but loving guides. His third-person narrators speak for the community, explaining why a boy's will must be restrained if he is ever to become a socially acceptable adult. On the other hand, Twain celebrates the child who refuses to compromise his integrity, creating a mythic otherworld as a substitute for the community for the child who reflects the author's own alienation from conventional ideas. These children—almost always first-person narrators —indicate Twain's ambivalence about the process of socialization by explicitly projecting values antithetical to those of the community. While his omniscient narrators reconcile the reader to the protagonist's socialization, his juvenile personae tempt the reader to believe there may be some way to live outside the community's rules. Moreover, these juvenile personae are the only children to experience the transcendent moments that make Mark Twain associate the notion of childhood with ecstatic possibilities rather than with merely mundane certainties. Only in flight from other people and their values can the solitary child discover his unity with the organic universe; the boy who tells his own story has left the moral confines of the town and found the spiritual freedom of the natural world. This child has a special kind of experience: a brief, intuited moment when he recognizes that his kinship to the organic world is spiritually more important than his ties to the human community.

These dual—and opposing—solutions to the conflict between the child and his society are most clearly illustrated by the contrast between the narrative method of *The Adventures of Tom Sawyer* and that of *The Adventures of Huckleberry Finn.* Narrated in the third person, *Tom Sawyer* conveys Twain's acknowledgment that it is necessary to socialize children; narrated in the first person, *Huck Finn* conveys Twain's intimation that the child who refuses enculturation will find compensation for his loneliness in the natural world around him.

The narrator of *Tom Sawyer* is both a moralist and a satirist, speaking as the former to children and as the latter to adults. His dual perspective, especially as regards the relationship between Tom and Aunt Polly, may explain why the book has always appealed to all age levels. As the narrator of a book for children, his task is largely didactic: to show that Tom, for all his mischief, must eventually take responsibility for his own actions; as the narrator of a book for adults, his task is redemptive: to help his readers remember their own rebellions against authority. Both tasks, notes Albert E. Stone, Jr., were customary among narrators of contemporary literature for and about children;[1] nonetheless, this narrator transcends his traditional functions. Because he mediates between character and reader, interceding time and again to tell the reader what significance an event bears to Tom or to Aunt Polly, he presents a private conflict within a social context, showing that Tom's struggle with Aunt Polly centers around his resistance to being socialized and implying that the boy must lose the battle because society's need for order is ultimately more important than Tom's need for independence.

The Adventures of Tom Sawyer may illustrate this aspect of familial tension better than any other single work in our literature. In order to show the emotional complexity of Tom and Aunt Polly's relationship, the narrator dramatizes the internal as well as the external battle of wills between his antagonists. For instance, Aunt Polly's response to her discovery that she had mistakenly punished Tom for breaking a sugar bowl would seem unreasonable if the narrator did not interpret her reasoning for us. Fearing that any concession would undermine her authority, she refuses to apologize to Tom; the narrator, however, hastily informs us that "her conscience reproached her, and she yearned to say something kind and loving; but she judged that this would be construed into a confession that she

1. Albert E. Stone, Jr., *The Innocent Eye: Childhood in Mark Twain's Imagination*, p. 63.

had been in the wrong, and discipline forbade that. So she kept silence, and went about her affairs with a troubled heart" (*TS*, p. 26).

Without narrative intercession it would be difficult to evaluate this adult's behavior as other than simple authoritarianism. When the narrator reports Aunt Polly's conflict, he encourages his audience to understand why she acts as she does. He helps us interpret her rigidity, first, within the context of her philosophy of child-rearing and, second, within the context of her intimate (if nonverbal) relationship with Tom. Indicating his emotional distance by employing a level of diction alien to both characters, the narrator demonstrates that, secretly, they understand each other. Having already made us more sympathetic to Aunt Polly, he makes us less so to Tom when he lets us know that the boy "sulked in a corner and exalted his woes. He knew that in her heart his aunt was on her knees to him, and he was morosely gratified by the consciousness of it" (*TS*, p. 26).

In addition to showing that adults are mindful of childrens' futures when they discipline them, scenes such as this also demonstrate that Mark Twain, though he was apt, as psychologist Robert R. Sears has noted, to dwell on incidents of separation anxiety and loss of love, nevertheless was keenly sensitive to the self-serving motives of the child.[2] Perhaps it will be useful to remember that when Twain wrote this novel he was already the father of two small children, the paterfamilias of a Victorian household where child-rearing was raised to a high art. He had ample opportunity to study his own children's behavior as well as to remember conflicts from the Hannibal days. When his narrator intercedes to reveal the characters' interior conflicts, he helps readers understand that Tom's self-pity is securely rooted in the boy's knowledge that his aunt loves him, even though she expresses her love in disciplinary terms. This is especially significant when we remember that Tom's destiny is to become a member of his community.[3] His secret knowledge

2. Robert R. Sears, "Mark Twain's Separation Anxiety," *Psychology Today* 13 (June 1979): 100–104.

3. In "The Sanctioned Rebel," Judith Fetterley examines Tom's relationship to the adults of the village, concluding that as the representative bad boy Tom has a symbiotic relationship with the adults, who, on the one hand, need his

that he is cherished defines the perimeters of his rebellion, shaping his conception of the social world he is being prepared to enter. Thematically, Tom and Aunt Polly's relationship concerns a child testing the limits of his developing ego and an adult continually checking her desire to indulge him by her knowledge that she must discipline in order to teach.[4]

Adventures of Huckleberry Finn, on the other hand, does not apologize for adult tyranny. Rather, it dismisses mediation altogether in order to focus on the child's immediate experience. Because the narrator is the child himself, the tension between him and his society is mediated only by the adult consciousness of the reader; *Huckleberry Finn* is not a book for children in part because a reader who fails to bring the "correct" set of values to it will fail to appreciate the moral lessons it holds. But moral lessons are cultural artifacts; they do not describe the essence of human nature. Prior to his socialization into a human group the child intuits his relationship to the organic world. Since in this novel Twain works directly through Huck's voice rather than using a third party to mediate between the protagonist and his experiences, he is forced to construct the world as Huck would see it, a task that can be accomplished only through imaginatively reencountering the world as the child originally encounters it. As we have seen, Huck is too unsophisticated to be able to stand back from the characters around him and judge moral issues according to some independent criterion. Similarly, he is too unsophisticated to stand back from the river landscape surrounding him and make studied remarks about it. His descriptions of both consequently give us an experience very close to his own. Even though Twain is carefully shaping his material, in these passages he is doing so through the eyes of his protagonist, suspending his own adult sense of social or historical context and reexperiencing the child's intense awareness of his environment.

According to Edith Cobb, "there is a special period, the little understood, prepubertal, halcyon, middle age of childhood . . .

---

energies as a break to the dullness of their lives and, on the other, see his emergence into maturity as affirmation of their values.

4. A standard work on early American attitudes toward children is Monica Kiefer, *American Children through their Books: 1700–1835.*

when the natural world is experienced in some highly evocative way, producing in the child a sense of some profound continuity with natural processes and presenting overt evidence of a biological basis of intuition."[5] During this period, according to Cobb, the child simultaneously experiences his first intimations of individuality and his innate kinship with nature. Out of his identification with nature emerges the intuitive grasp of the world that the Romantics saw as poetic genius and to which they claimed to return in memory in order to renew their creative impulse. For Cobb, it is only through a return to the sense of integration with the processes of nature that the poet can retrieve his spiritual past; she points out that the Romantic poets "returned" by remembering periods during their youths when they had left their homes to wander in solitary communion with nature. Or, in the words of Bachelard, "Childhood knows unhappiness through men . . . when the human world leaves him in peace, the child feels like the son of the cosmos."[6] The immediacy with which Huck communicates his happiness at returning to the river shows an author retrieving the cosmic consciousness of the child in an almost willful abandonment of adult context. Forsaking the omniscient narrator, in *Huck Finn* Mark Twain trades mediation for immediate engagement, thus retrieving both the anguish and the joy of the child's encounters with men and nature.

In order to show how Twain retrieves the solitary child's sensibility, and how only the solitary child experiences Twain's special moments of childhood, it will be useful to again compare parallel incidents in *The Adventures of Tom Sawyer* and *Adventures of Huckleberry Finn*. In both novels the protagonists have what we may call a meditation scene, a period during which they feel abused and go off to muse about their troubles. The rhetorical differences between the two passages illustrate how Twain's retrieval of childhood through a third-person narrator forces him to accept the necessity of the child's enculturation, while his retrieval of childhood through allowing the child narrator to relate his own experiences permits the author to create a narrative environment through which he can demonstrate his sense of the child's capacity for ecstasy.

5. Edith Cobb, "The Ecology of Imagination in Childhood," p. 538.
6. Gaston Bachelard, *The Poetics of Reverie: Childhood, Language, and the Cosmos*, p. 100.

In *Tom Sawyer*, after Tom's "day of grief"—the same day Aunt Polly unjustly punishes him—he goes and sits by the river to nurse his wounds and to daydream about his new (and unreciprocated) love for Becky Thatcher. The narrator tells us that wandering "far from the accustomed haunts of boys," Tom "sought desolate places that were in harmony with his spirit. A log raft in the river invited him, and he seated himself on its outer edge and contemplated the dreary vastness of the stream." Wondering if Becky, informed of his plight, "would . . . cry, and wish . . . to put her arms around his neck and comfort him" or whether she would "turn coldly away, like all the hollow world," Tom indulges in his fantasy until "he wore it threadbare. At last he rose up sighing and departed in the darkness" *(TS*, p. 27).

Much of the appeal of this passage stems from the narrator's manipulation of rhetorical conventions as he communicates Tom's thoughts. As part of a chapter that might well be titled "Tom's Day of Woe," the boy's plight—his entrapment by his love for and resentment of two women—is treated as comic material. Conscious of Tom's propensity for self-dramatization, the narrator demonstrates his disengagement from Tom's emotions by couching Tom's vision of his world in language most suited to the genre of the sentimental novel, where adult heroes are permitted a wide latitude of overt subjectivity as they face exaggerated issues of life and death. One of the reasons writers like William Dean Howells disapproved of sentimental novels was that they taught young readers to think such self-absorption permissible;[7] in rhetorically associating Tom's misery with sentimental heroes in similar plights, the narrator of *Tom Sawyer* undermines the validity of his protagonist's emotion. Furthermore, he increases his distance from Tom's self-pity through the rounded rhetorical structure of the paragraph: Tom "sought desolate places" in the opening sentence and "departed in darkness" in the last. The body of the paragraph paraphrases Tom's thoughts and the paths they traverse; his meditation "away from the haunts of boys" seeks nature only as the setting appropriate for nursing his social wounds. This may be the most

7. William Dean Howells, "Realism: The Moral Issue," in *W. D. Howells as*

self-consciously "constructed" passage in the novel; the combination of high diction and rounded paragraph structure high-
lights Twain's parody of the hero in distress.

In contrast to the melodramatic style employed by the narrator of *Tom Sawyer*, Huck never uses high diction. In addition, he
rarely conveys overt self-pity. Even when he is "lonesome,"
Huck tries not to dwell on himself; consequently, the only way
we can usually divine his emotional state is through objective
correlatives: having told us that he "felt so lonesome I most
wisht I was dead" in his room at the Widow's, he hears the
creatures of the woods as echoes of his own psychic state:

> The stars was shining, and the leaves rustled in the woods ever so
> mournful; and I heard an owl, away off, who-whooing about some-
> body that was dead, and a whippowill and a dog crying about
> somebody that was going to die, and the wind was trying to whisper
> something to me and I couldn't make out what it was, and so it made
> the cold shivers run over me. (*HF*, p. 5)

This scene concludes a "Day of Woe" for Huck as miserable as
Tom's day: both have lost power struggles with the adults who
control them. While the difference in their responses partly
reflects the differences in their characters—Tom lives in a
fantasy world constructed from his literary sources, whereas
Huck is rooted in the empirical present—it also demonstrates
how Twain uses the two narrative points of view to recall
distinct moments of childhood. Tom's fantasies achieve universal truth and gain the reader's sympathy because they are
paraphrased and interpreted by a third party; had we heard Tom
himself tell us about them they could never have achieved the
cultural significance the narrator can give them by linking them
to the fantasies of all children undergoing the traumas of socialization.[8] Huck's meditation, in contrast, retrieves a past in
which the solitary child finds the echoes of his own emotions in
the woods and fields about him. While Tom's ego seeks its

Critic, edited by Edwin H. Cady (London and Boston: Routledge & Kegan Paul,
1973), pp. 97–103.

8. In addition, as Stone notes, even though Tom's reading has given a
"literary cast" to his speech and thoughts, a careful look at Tom's own speeches
in both *Tom Sawyer* and *Huckleberry Finn* shows that Twain was careful not to

reflection in society, generating fantasies wherein he vengefully manipulates those who oppose him, Huck's ego seeks its reflection in the natural world, becoming increasingly conscious of its relationship to organic processes. Tom wants revenge for his injuries, but Huck only seeks escape from their source; his death wishes are not means to inflict pain on others, only a way to put an end to his own. Emotionally, one senses, Huck perceives himself as a part of nature, and he signals his rejection of society through his embrace of nature imagery.

In addition, there is little rhetorical rounding exhibited in Huck's narrative. The passage quoted above is part of a long paragraph that begins with Huck's conflicts with Miss Watson and ends with him accidentally killing a spider, a sign, to him, of bad luck. This is not to say that the paragraph lacks structure; rather, each sentence brilliantly develops another facet of Huck's loneliness, frustration, and superstition. But since Huck is doing the developing, the self-consciously rounded narrative precision of the passage from *Tom Sawyer* is missing. Since Huck's goal is to tell his story rather than to teach a lesson, he does not have to be self-conscious about his style. In fact, Huck's lack of narrative self-consciousness is what makes him capable of communicating ecstasy; his preferred image can only be communicated by narrative immediacy.

The contrast between the arbitrary divisions of time imposed by the town and the atemporality offered by nature frames Twain's special moments of childhood. The dichotomy suggests that he saw the unsocialized child as a being oblivious to temporal distinctions. In the Mississippi valley pieces especially, escapes from the community resemble escapes into timeless realms where the subject engages in a world that is inviting precisely because in its organic continuity it abrogates the community's idea that time must be broken up and utilized. Since the conflict between self and society exhibited in these stories often centers around the child's resistance to the community's control over the way he spends his time, the triumph of civilization can be seen as the production of a being who only

---

let his young protagonist grasp his sources too carefully. He borrows key terms and plots, but he misuses words and confuses scenes.

spends his time in useful, that is, pecuniarily productive, work. The child, however, rebels against subordinating himself to these rules. In his periods of escape from the town he finds his true being in a natural setting where he loses his always tenuous sense of time. It is significant that Tom is constantly being punished for arriving home late; as soon as he leaves the village he ceases to be conscious of its temporal divisions. Moreover, Huck is most depressed by the way his time is regulated during the months he spends with the Widow. When, in *Huck Finn*, he remembers that "you had to eat on a plate, and go to bed and get up regular" (*HF*, p. 22), he is only repeating his complaint in *Tom Sawyer* that she "makes me get up just at the same time every morning . . . the widder eats by a bell; she goes to bed by a bell; she gets up by a bell—everything's so awful reg'lar a body can't stand it" (*TS*, p. 216). Thus, when Twain came to write the story of his unconventional boy, he did not need to view his protagonist within his social or historical context. By letting Huck speak for himself, Twain develops a point of view that is by its very nature ahistorical.

Whereas the narrator of *Tom Sawyer* uses a high diction, when Twain weds the vernacular to Huck's point of view he creates a prose that conveys the ahistorical sensibility of his speaker by forcing the reader to suspend adult consciousness, reexperiencing what it is like to be a child inhabiting the sensual world as a being integral to it. This world is not always idyllic—unsophisticated minds experience fear as intensely as they do joy—but it is authentic; it returns us to encounters unmediated by our own enculturation. When Huck describes the landscape of the river we sense the authorial energy invested in re-creating his sense of timelessness. After he and Jim breakfasted, Huck recalls,

> we would watch the lonesomeness of the river, and kind of lazy along, and by-and-by lazy off to sleep . . . then for about an hour there wouldn't be nothing to hear nor nothing to see—just solid lonesomeness. Next you'd see a raft sliding by, away off yonder, and maybe a galoot on it chopping, because they're most always doing it on a raft; you'd see that ax go up again, and by the time it's above the man's head, then you hear the *k'chunk*—it had took all

that time to come over the river. So we would put in the day, lazying around, listening to the stillness. *(HF,* p. 100)

Fluctuating between a continuing past tense and a present tense, Huck indicates how little the environment ever really changes; in addition, "because they're most always doing it on a raft" describes the comfortable routine that life on the river follows, while "lazying around, listening to the stillness" renders Huck's criteria for contentment in a life free of the strident demands of the community. Because the detail here is built entirely from Huck's perceptions, and because it is not distorted by being forced into the language of conventional landscape description, it is as close to the objects themselves as any verbal representation of a material thing can be. Through the medium of vernacular language, Twain sees the world through the eyes of the child who perceives it; through the grammatical scrambling of tenses, he shows that out on the river even man-centered events lose their uniqueness and become part of the natural cycle.

Thus, while the narrator of *Tom Sawyer* regards his protagonist's rebellion from the community's point of view, as a temporary flight from regulations that are necessary even if they are restrictive, the narrator of *Huck Finn* regards his own rebellion as an escape from meaningless restrictions. For Huck, the river environment is good simply because it does not substitute arbitrary rhythms for natural ones. Because he lacks an adult narrator's emotional or temporal distance from the material he is writing about, Huck can only report his acts from his own point of view; his narrative, consequently, conveys the easy lyricism of a soul unselfconsciously recording its own journey.

For Mark Twain, constructing Huck's voice meant suspending his own sense of adult context, moving himself by rhetorical means beyond a historical or didactic sensibility into an atemporal region of the psyche where he could retrieve the past through a reverie akin to the reveries of a child. Having achieved this through the freedom of the vernacular in *Adventures of Huckleberry Finn*, Twain discovered that he could escape his own anxieties by using a first-person narrator who could rhetorically retrieve the child's sensibilities. For instance, in his

Autobiography, composed long after the magic of Huck's voice had failed him, the first-person narrator still has the power to re-create the past. At the end of his reminiscences about the Quarles Farm, where he spent much time as a child, Twain moves into an extended passage whose oneiric lyricism depends on repetitions beginning with "I can see," "I can feel," "I know," "I can call back." Once more the theme concerns a child's experiences of the natural world through the senses. In order to recall his own experiences Twain approaches his memories through a series of incantatory phrases, juxtaposing the "I" of this passage to the predominant "I" of the book, that is, to the voice of a man reflecting on his own past within its historical context. The rhythmic structure of the incantatory passage signals a sudden shift from the external world to the internal; through this shift, the dreamer insists that he "can call it all back and make it as real as it ever was, and as blessed."[9]

In "calling it back," the writer re-creates a series of precise sensory images as his young sensibilities responded to them. Each image is projected outward from the consciousness that perceives it; each is an entity experienced in isolation before it becomes a part of the whole. "I know the stain of blackberries," the writer tells us, and "can see the blue clusters of wild grapes." "I can feel the thumping rain, upon my head, of hickory nuts," he remembers, and "I know the taste of maple sap." Most of these recalled images are prefaced by the phrase "I know"; the solitary child's wisdom is built, Lockean fashion, from his experiences of the external world. In addition, Twain's use of the present tense reinforces his thematic insistence that he can "call back" the past; in this passage grammatical detemporalization joins rhythmic incantation, suggesting an entranced state during which the dreamer feels that he is reviving his kinship to the cosmos. Within that context, peace is equated with solitude and stasis: "I can call back the prairie," he tells us, "and its loneliness and peace, and a vast hawk hanging motionless in the sky."[10] When he abandons the adult world, the speaker rediscovers his childhood self through the agency of the sensory world that he recalls. And like Huck's transformation of

9. Albert Bigelow Paine, ed., *Mark Twain's Autobiography,* p. 110.
10. Ibid.

the particular into the eternal through the scrambling of tenses, Mark Twain's transformation of the past into the present through the repetition of present-tense constructions creates an immutable otherworld in which the speaker, no matter in which period of actual time he is writing, can escape his anxieties and feel at one with the universe.

Other of Twain's stories of childhood exhibit the difference he felt between the child's experiences as they are interpreted by a third party and the child's experiences as only the subject can report them. In *The Prince and the Pauper*, the historical novel Twain wrote especially for children, narrative intrusion functions as it does in *Tom Sawyer*, creating distances of emotion and time between reader, author, and character and thus helping the reader to interpret cultural gaps. Here, too, the narrator paraphrases the protagonists' responses, thus forcing the reader to experience an emotion vicariously rather than firsthand. For instance, when the little king, seeking shelter in a dark barn for the night, suspects he is bedded down next to a fresh corpse, he is subjected to the same narrative indirection and condescension to which Tom had been subjected during his day of woe: "It was a grisly thing, this light touch from this noiseless invisible presence; it made the boy sick with ghostly fears. What should he do? . . . Should he leave these reasonably comfortable quarters and fly from this inscrutable horror? . . . No . . . he must . . . find that thing" *(P&P*, p. 120).

After he discovers that the "presence" is a sleeping calf the king is "cordially ashamed of himself . . . but he need not have felt so about it, for it was not the calf that frightened him but a dreadful nonexistent something which the calf stood for; and any other boy in those old superstitious times would have acted and suffered just as he had done" *(P&P*, p. 121). Here we see two fairly typical purposes at work in Twain's tales: to tell a hair-raising ghost story, at which he excelled, and to "explode" the story in order to teach young readers how to dispel their own "superstitious" terrors. Consequently, this passage, while stimulating childhood fears of the dark, also proves that—like the rest of childhood fantasies—such fears are groundless in light of the "adult" world of reason and empirical investigation.

In the manuscript fragment "Huck Finn and Tom Sawyer Among the Indians," in contrast, the first-person narration does not permit third party intrusion. Huck, the narrator, lets Tom tell about one of his own experiences; instead of being manipulated by the careful pacing necessary to create the progressive tension of a ghost story, the reader is confronted by Tom's own disjointed record of his terror. When he first realized he was lost in the fog, Tom tells Huck,

> I begun to tremble all over, and I did wish the fog would lift, but it didn't, it shut me in, all around, like a thick white smoke. I wanted to wait, and let you miss me and come back, but I couldn't stay still a second; it would a killed me; I *had* to run, and I did. And so I kept on running, by the hour, and listening, and shouting; but never a sound did ever I hear; and whenever I stopped just a moment and held my breath to listen, it was the awfulest stillness that ever was, and I couldn't stand it and had to run on again. ("HTI," p. 128)

Here Tom records his panic in a series of polysyndetic conjuncts, a strategy of overusing conjunctions for rhetorical effect that Twain often employs to indicate intensity in a child. In this passage the conjunctions communicate Tom's loss of control. Whereas in *The Prince and the Pauper* the narrator intruded first to frighten his readers by referring to the rhetorical conventions of the Gothic suspense story ("But to stay where he was and endure this living death all night?") and then to teach a useful lesson ("he thought these false thoughts because he did not know the immortal strength of human curiosity"), the lack of narrative mediation in "Huck and Tom Among the Indians" prevents such overt didacticism. We know—as Tom does—that he should have stayed in one place and let his friends find him; the passage, however, does not seek to tell us what we already know. Rather, it seeks to communicate the psychic experiences of an ordinarily level-headed child who panics. In doing so it indicates another means of suspending adult context: panic is one way that we can recall some of our original experiences of the world as chaos. As Tom continues his story his sentences lengthen and his phrases shorten; while he never altogether loses his ability to reason, he becomes increasingly paranoid, convinced that every sign of life he sees indicates an enemy rather than a friend. Although his tale ends on a fairly humorous note, his recitation verges on the hysterical. Through Tom's fragments we become engaged in his experience of loss and terror; we perceive the world through an increasingly disoriented consciousness.

While none of Louis de Conte's observations in *Joan of Arc* is so stripped of literary conventions as to function as an original encounter, he, too, recalls his childhood idyll and his association with the "marvelous child" who became Saint Joan by suspending his adult sense of historical context through rhetorical means. Like most of Twain's passages designed to evoke an idyllic era in the past, the language used in de Conte's preface suggests that time passes as a flowing, or funneling, of continuous experience rather than as a series of discrete entities. "As the years and the decades drifted by, and the spectacle of the marvelous child's meteor-flight across the war-firmament of France . . . receded deeper and deeper into the past and grew ever more strange, and wonderful, and divine, and pathetic, I came to comprehend and recognize her at last for what she was—the most noble life that was ever born into this world save only One" *(JA,* 1:xvi). Only through time (as distance) can de Conte understand Joan's stature in the world; only through abolishing time, however, can he retrieve the magic of his years with her.

In addition to evoking memories of Joan through language that suggests a funneling into the past, de Conte also employs those key adjectives and nouns that signify spiritual respite in Twain's work, suggesting the protagonist's entry into a landscape where "dreaming," "serenity," and "contentment" are synonymous with the abolition of time. The tree, especially, is recalled through references to visions or dreams. For de Conte it exists simultaneously on two temporal planes: in the past, as the representative of his happy childhood, and in the future, as the promise of his salvation. When he recalls the halcyon days of Domremy, de Conte tells us that the song of the tree "has gone murmuring through my dreaming spirit all my life when I was weary and troubled, resting me and carrying me through night and distance home again" *(JA,* 1:29). Similarly, bridging the decades separating him from his childhood, he reports, "I . . . wait [for Death] with serenity; for I have seen the vision of the Tree. I have seen it, and am content" *(JA,* 1:29). For de Conte, death promises a renewal of his childhood serenity because it, too, will be ruled by the presence of the tree and it, too, will be characterized by a state of spiritual tranquillity.

Perhaps one of the reasons Twain was so pleased with *Joan* was that it is the only novel in which he takes his protagonists from childhood to adulthood, that is, across the threshold of history. For most readers, however, this is where the narrative voice fails. As soon as de Conte begins to recount the history of Joan's treatment by the Church his voice is no longer that of a contemporary but becomes that of Mark Twain. The tension Twain tries to construct between de Conte's fidelity to Joan, on the one hand, and to his medieval, Catholic worldview on the other becomes a major problem of narrative consistency; the result is a narrator who can express only two emotions: outrage and nostalgia. He cannot achieve a detached view of the history he is recording, as an omniscient, mediating, narrator could have done, but he is too far removed from the naiveté of childhood to display the innate mixture of sadness, perplexity, and insight displayed by Huck. Consequently, he records the injustices of the trial and, when these memories become too painful, escapes back to his earlier ones, to childhood, the peacefulness of nature, the tree, all images that are in stark contrast to the corruption of the historical moment. Of his subsequent adult life we learn nothing. Rather, we leap from his outraged chronicle to his testimony of old age and bitterness; in the end, as at the beginning, we meet a misanthrope who not even Joan's restitution has sufficed to reconcile to his time. Alone in his grasp of ultimate truths, de Conte remains loyal only to his private memories. Because there is no third-person voice in this novel, there is no sympathetic other who can help de Conte absorb his shock and accept the mistakes of his contemporaries, recognizing, as an adult must, that all men are fallible. Consequently, although de Conte survives his immediate historical crisis, he never escapes his spiritual one; the alienation that began with the circumstances of his birth rules his vision of the society he now desires only to castigate and escape.

The major difference between Twain's omniscient third-person narrators and his juvenile personae is that despite his own contention, in the case of Tom Sawyer, that if he took his protagonist into manhood "he would lie like all the one-horse men in literature and the reader would conceive a hearty contempt for him,"[11] the third-person narrator does provide a framework for his protagonist's maturity. Since he has already guided his hero onto the footpath of history, the detached narrator could, if Twain wished, lead him through its labyrinth. This was decidedly not Twain's goal, of course. He cherished the imaginative power of his young heroes precisely because it was perishable; it is the genius of the narrator of *Tom Sawyer* to communicate the fragility of the child's sensibility even while he anticipates its destruction. For Twain, moreover, the special moment of childhood occurred when a child perceived his intimacy with the organic world. During that moment the child, conscious of himself as unlike other people, still saw himself as part of the uncorrupted universe; he recognized his own individuality as part of a greater unity. When Huck finds objective correlatives in the woods to express his fears or joys, he reflects the speaker of Wordsworth's *Prelude*, to whom "Coercing all things into sympathy / To unorganic nature were transferred / My own enjoyments."[12] Because their responses are unmediated, Twain's first-person juvenile personae can express this fragile unity; conversely, his omniscient third-person narrators, in being cognizant that the child's communion with nature is a subject for discussion, are a priori detached from that communion. By mating the child's unselfconscious perceptions of his organic environment with the freedom of the vernacular, Twain creates a narrative where, in Conrad Aiken's lines, "The landscape and the language are the same, / And we ourselves are language and are land."[13]

Finally, the first-person narrators cannot "grow up" because their creativity is inseparable from their lack of perspective on themselves and the world around them. The omniscient narra-

11. Henry Nash Smith and William M. Gibson, eds., with the assistance of Frederick Anderson, *Mark Twain-Howells Letters: The Correspondence of Samuel L. Clemens and William D. Howells, 1872–1910*, 1: 92.

12. William Wordsworth, *The Prelude*, book I, lines 390–92.

13. Conrad Aiken, Poem #XI, in *A Letter from Li Po and Other Poems* (New York: Oxford University Press, 1955), p. 27.

tor, understanding his protagonist's bewilderment, ean rationalize its necessity for his readers. The first-person child narrator, however, has no one to whom he can shift that burden, no guide to mediate between him, the community, and the reader; his narrative style, consequently, is as unstudied, as naive, as are his assessments of what is happening. In order to maintain his reliability, however, he must never gain perspective on himself. For Twain the crucial determinant of the child's continued unselfconsciousness seems to be participation in an act of oppression. If he consciously helps hurt someone else, he destroys his unity with the natural world, a type of fall from grace most often represented by participation in (as distinct from observation of) mob action. Those who merely observe, like Huck, escape back to their spiritual sanctuaries with expressions of disgust for human nature; those who participate, like Theodor in "The Chronicle of Young Satan," remain in the town and try to rationalize their disgust at themselves. For Twain, however, as soon as a character experiences self-loathing he becomes conscious of himself as an object; therefore he can no longer be a participant in a state of subjective grace. If his story continues much past the character's fall, Twain's difficulties with maintaining a consistent narrative voice almost inevitably appear. As soon as the child becomes a man he reflects the division of consciousness between participant and observer that ruled the life of his creator.

Retrieving the period before he lost his own childlike unity with the natural world became one of Twain's chief means of escaping his own tensions. His first-person narrators illustrate his ability to use language as a means of retrieving that period, a capacity Wordsworth saw as "the first / Poetic Spirit of our human life; / By uniform control of after years / In most abated or suppressed, in some, / Pre-eminent till death."[14] Choosing to participate in history, Twain still harbored a desire to escape it. The image of the child in intuitive communion with nature was one way he retrieved a past that stood beyond the terrors of corruption, self-hatred, and change.

---

14. Wordsworth, *The Prelude*, book II, lines 260–65.

7

Women: The Imagery of Protection

Olivia Langdon, whom Mark Twain married in 1870, was the prototype for the women he celebrates in his fiction. Even his image of Livy, however, reflects an artistic quest to create an ideality from an actuality. When Sam Clemens met Livy Langdon late in 1867, he was a world-traveled author of thirty-two, she a provincial of twenty-one. Their courtship was largely conducted by mail since Twain was at that time making his living by lecturing throughout the northeastern United States. Through his letters Twain projected the woman he wanted Livy to be; because he was sitting in hotel rooms fantasizing her rather than actually conversing with her, he could create the woman and the relationship he wanted just as he could create any other fictional situation. He was able to transform a real woman into an ideal one by shaping contemporary stereotypes of the good woman to fit his particular needs.

It is clear from Twain's courtship letters that even before they were married he associated Livy with an escape from the lecture circuit that he had already grown to loathe and with recovery of the familial warmth and harmony he claimed to have lost when he began his wanderings as a journeyman printer in 1853. Furthermore, the rhetorical overflow of these letters is the first sign of his propensity to drift into sentimental effusions whenever he wrote to or about a gentle young woman. When he assured Livy that even if she left her home to marry him she would "not know this great blank, this awful vacancy, this *something missed, something lost*"[1] that he had experienced since leaving his mother's house, he was also assuring himself that through Livy he would regain the "refuge from care" that a part of him craved. Utilizing references to bodies of water,

1. *Mark Twain's Collected Letters*, vol. 1, 1853–1869, edited by Lin Salamo, #251.

already associated with profound peace and contentment in his writings, Twain told Livy on New Year's Eve 1868 that the old year "found me a waif, floating at random on the sea of life, and it leaves me freighted with a good purpose, and blessed with a fair wind, a chart to follow, a port to reach . . . and I, the homeless, then have on this last day of the dying year, a home that is priceless, a refuge from all the cares and ills of life, in that warm heart of yours, and am supremely happy!"[2] And the next day he remarked to Joseph Twichell, "Ours is a funny correspondence, and a mighty satisfactory one, altogether. My letters are an ocean of love in a storm—hers an ocean of love in the majestic repose of a great calm. But the waters are the same, just the same, my boy."[3]

At the same time that he sought familial warmth and domestic harmony by courting an avowedly conventional girl, however, Twain also intimated the other function that conventional households served in his emotional life. Claiming to crave stability, and adopting substitute mothers as he traveled across the country, he nonetheless regarded the "homes" they provided as places where he could be "just as troublesome as I want to," being permitted "to smoke in the house, & bring in snow on my boots, & sleep late, & eat at unseasonable hours, & leave my valise wide open on the floor and my soiled linen about it . . . I tell you I *like* that. It is being at *home*, you know."[4] Here Twain is demanding to be the exception to the domestic rule, permitted to flout the very regulations necessary for the harmony he says he is seeking. After he left the West, Twain never seriously suggested that he would like to return to the vagabond life of the frontier, but the personal habits he indulged there must have been emblems of freedom for him. To be permitted to indulge those habits in a society where other people observed the conventions expressed his sense of his public self exactly: he wanted to be seen as the outlaw from conventional society who is so irresistible that conventional people will love him despite his flagrant misbehavior. Much as Tom Sawyer's relationship with his aunt defined the limits of his rebellion, the loving admonitions of Twain's coterie of loyal women gave him the

2. Ibid., #258.
3. Ibid., #259.
4. Dixon Wecter, ed., *Mark Twain to Mrs. Fairbanks*, p. 54.

security he needed to commit his heresies. When he turned his older friend Mary Fairbanks into an "overbearing mother," and Livy Langdon into a "watchful wife," he constructed the parameters of his own public rebellions. As the perpetual "Youth" (Livy's nickname for him), Sam Clemens could be the perpetual bad boy in the guise of the fictional character named Mark Twain, and in fact he managed to enact this role for years within his own household (and within that of the Howellses): pacing around the room talking while everyone else ate lunch, smoking his customary ten cigars a day, playing billiards until past midnight, and ragging the butler in public.

Clearly his nonconformity—in which he delighted—could not have existed without an established order against which he could exhibit it, and obtaining this order was his goal when he was courting Livy. In summarizing a letter he had written to Twichell, Twain told Livy, "What we want is a *home*—we are done with the shows & vanities of life & are ready to enter upon its realities—we are tired of chasing its phantoms & shadows, & are ready to grasp its substance. At least *I* am—& 'I' means both of us, & 'both of us' means I of course—for are not we Twain one flesh?"[5] Using his stage name to hide his seriousness, Twain accomplishes several purposes here: to tell Livy what he expects her to want, to strengthen his association of her with home, and to absorb her into the manifold splits in his personality. The playful tone and clichéd language do not disguise the real message of this letter, which is that the Clemenses' home will constitute the core of Mark Twain's life, the innermost circle of the sphere around which his multiple personalities will revolve. As his wife, Livy will provide the stability that his public life lacks; to her he will retreat when his anxieties threaten to overwhelm him and from her he will rebel when his confidence returns.

The ideal woman into which Twain made Livy reflects not only his peculiar needs, however, it reflects contemporary stereotypes as well. Four years after their marriage Twain wrote to Livy from Salisbury, England: "To-day I attended the grand Christmas service in Salisbury Cathedral. . . . And then we drove by Old Sarum—all day I was thinking lovingly of my

5. Ibid., p. 73n.

'Angel in the House'—for Old Sarum and Salisbury recal [sic] Coventry Patmore's books."[6]

Twain's comparison of Livy to the woman in Patmore's popular poem "The Angel in the House" illustrates the mold into which he cast his young wife: he saw her as gentle, pure, and inspiring. Furthermore, when he recalls Patmore's poem he implicitly compares his relationship to his wife to the relationship the poem's speaker bears toward his "Angel," regarding her as his moral and temperamental superior. Part of Twain's courtship strategy in 1868–1869 had been to persuade Livy that she could redeem him from his wayward life through her faith and goodness; throughout his life he praised her for being finer, stronger, and more sensitive than he. More than anything else, his letters to her show that he thought of her as his emotional and moral complement.

In "Victorian Masculinity and the Angel in the House," Carol Christ, examining Tennyson's as well as Patmore's images of women, notes that both poets reveal their own ambivalence about male aggressions by stressing passive females, and she claims that the poem was popular with both sexes because in the course of paying tribute to the good woman it helped male readers recognize that their own anxieties were normal.[7] In addition, I suggest, Patmore's poem helped Victorians transcend their anxieties through its celebration of marriage. At least since the Greeks sexual love has been associated with wholeness in the Western mind; avoiding the explicitly sexual, Victorians transferred the notion of fulfillment to domestic concerns. "Each [sex] has what the other has not," claims John Ruskin in "Of Queens Gardens." "Each completes the other, and is completed by the other: they are in nothing alike, and the happiness and perfection of both depend on each asking and receiving from the other what the other only can give."[8] As Walter E. Houghton has noted, "Of Queens Gardens" is the fullest articulation of the sexual vision of the age;[9] even Ruskin's vocabulary, which transforms opposition into complementarity, illustrates a quest

6. Alan Gribben, *Mark Twain's Library: A Reconstruction*, 2: 536.
7. Carol Christ, "Victorian Masculinity and the Angel in the House."
8. John Ruskin, *Sesame and Lilies*, pp. 58–59.
9. Walter E. Houghton, *The Victorian Frame of Mind, 1830–1870*.

for psychic unity through marriage. Subjected to what Ruskin called the "anxieties of the outer life," or what Mark Twain called the "driving, toiling, world outside,"[10] the Victorian man tended to consider his home "a sacred place, a vestal temple." When he retreated to his home, he retreated to a sphere removed from economic "progress" and therefore emotionally outside the chaos of history. The living heart of his home, his woman symbolized stability, continuity, and peace.

Within this context, Twain's idealization of Livy and of most of the wives in his fiction reflects a cultural tendency to make women into symbols of spiritual respite. As always in his writing, however, Twain not only reshaped popular images but also continually redefined those appearing in his earlier works so that they kept pace with the development of his other thematic concerns. Within the themes that he developed in his fiction, his female characters fall into three main categories: older, unmarried women tend to be guardians of the protagonists' consciences; younger, unmarried women tend to be moral exemplars; and married women of all ages tend to be homemakers whose most important function is to provide an environment wherein their husbands can find spiritual and physical respite from the stress of their public lives. In his late work, however, Twain expands the married women's caretaking role to include protecting their husbands from the results of their own self-absorption, helping them maintain their sanity as well as providing them with a tranquil environment. In these works the protagonist looks to his wife to correct his perceptions when he suspects he is dreaming because he believes that her consciousness is rooted in the empirical world, while his has a tendency to drift off into fantasies. The development of this function among Twain's fictional wives parallels similar developments in his relationship with Livy; as Twain aged he tended increasingly to depend on Livy to provide him with the emotional stability he could not obtain himself. Furthermore, Twain's sense that wives existed to help their husbands discriminate between fantasies and realities originated in his other female characters: young or old, Twain's good woman con-

10. Wecter, ed., *To Mrs. Fairbanks*, p. 61n.

stantly reminds the male protagonist that he must stop acting as if he were the only consciousness in existence.

The women who have been most studied in Twain's fiction are those who function as foils for a young protagonist's adventures. Sexless and rigidly conventional, they are a far cry from the loving wife he ultimately celebrated. Nevertheless, they constitute the first development of that preferred image. One of the traditional functions of the Angel of the House was to remind her man of his higher nature, to teach him the virtue of altruism; in Twain's early work this job is performed by the aunt or widow who spends her life caring for others. Variations on the "watchdog" stereotype into which Twain turned Mrs. Fairbanks and, often, Livy, this figure initiates the protagonist's education in social accountability.

As we saw in Chapter 6, the function of the female authority figure in Twain's novels about children is to teach her charge the values of his society. Mark Twain, however, only partly subscribed to those values; consequently, the older women in his novels about childhood are as much foils for his own ambivalence as they are for his protagonists' adventures. He partly resolves his ambivalence by classifying the "aunt" figure according to whether she tries to control the boys (and, occasionally, men) for the sheer pleasure it gives her to exercise authority, or whether she does so as a means of helping them mature. The characters who perform their duties simply because they relish power fail to be moral guides. Miss Watson, for instance, tries to sell Jim down the river, condemns Huck because he is oblivious to the importance of manners, and says he is stupid because he does not understand that her clichés about the power of prayer are figurative rather than literal. When she finally tells him, "It was wicked to say what I said; said she wouldn't say it for the whole world; *she* was going to live so as to go to the good place," he declares his rebellion by deciding, "I couldn't see no advantage in going where she was going, so I made up my mind I wouldn't try for it" *(HF,* p. 4). Since she is unimaginative, rude, and hypocritical, Huck rejects her values along with her pretensions to authority over him.

Similarly, in "The Facts Concerning the Recent Carnival of

Crime in Connecticut," the authoritarian personality of the woman who tries to reform the narrator undermines her mission. Here, consciences are personified and characterized as growing large or small according to the amount of exercise they are given. When Aunt Mary, whose conscience "lives in the open air altogether, because no door is large enough to admit her" ("FCCC," p. 126), begins lecturing the protagonist (whose conscience is small enough to sit on a bookshelf), she does not give his conscience any opportunity to expand. Her moral largess is a disguise for authoritarian prowess; she obviously enjoys itemizing her nephew's faults more than she would enjoy observing his virtues. While she is berating him for his lack of charity, however, he is gleefully watching his conscience shrivel, until it "droop[ed] languidly to the floor, blinking toward me a last supplication for mercy, with heavy eyes" ("FCCC," p. 128). As soon as it falls asleep, he kills it and cheerfully banishes Aunt Mary's "pestilent morals" for ever. Like Miss Watson, Aunt Mary does not succeed in reforming the protagonist because she is more concerned to impose her will on him than to help him understand the importance of sacrificing his own desires for the common good.

Aunt Polly and the Widow Douglas, on the other hand, are representative of the female authority figures who fall within Twain's classification of the good woman. The women who do succeed in becoming moral guides for Twain's boys appeal to the protagonists' sympathies instead of simply preaching at them. Furthermore, their own generosity comes from the heart rather than the conscience. Both Aunt Polly and the Widow secretly sympathize with their young charges, appreciating their energy and creative potential. The Widow even understands the importance of praise in guiding a child in the right direction: she partly wins Huck's loyalties when she tells him he "was coming along slow but sure, and doing very satisfactory. She said she warn't ashamed of me" (*HF*, p. 15). Most of Twain's good women influence their charges' moral growth by pointing out how much their misbehavior hurts those who care for them. When Aunt Polly chides Tom for having let her think he was dead, she reminds him, "You think to come all the way over here from Jackson's Island in the night to laugh at our troubles . . . but you couldn't even think to pity us and save us from sorrow" *(TS,* p. 127). Huck's moral growth is generally achieved through Jim's agency, but near the end of the last section of the novel, commonly referred to as the Evasion episode, after he and Tom have tortured the Phelps family with their pranks, when Aunt Sally begs him not to run away during the night "for *my* sake," Huck realizes, "Laws knows I *wanted* to go, bad enough . . . and was intending to go; but after that, I wouldn't a went, not for kingdoms" *(HF,* p. 236). For both boys, the women's heartfelt pleas penetrate where mere authoritarian demands cannot.

These women provide the stability out of which Twain's young protagonists emerge. They are the guardians—perhaps even the creators—of moral order among men. When the protagonists rebel against them, they are overtly protesting adult rules, but covertly protesting the adult demand that the boys think of something beyond their own pleasures. The women's most important function is to ask the boys to make the first movement outside their own egos, to adopt another person's viewpoint and to recognize that other people also can experience pain. As Huck grows morally by learning to see that Jim, too, has feelings, so other young protagonists develop moral principles by having older women point out that their pranks can hurt as well as amuse other people. Despite their own limitations (they would not believe Jim has feelings, either), the women are aware that the first requisite for community is that individuals learn to regulate their own behavior. One of the indications of their importance as backdrops for the protagonists' adventures is that when they are absent Twain's dramatization flounders. In *Tom Sawyer Abroad* and *Huck and Tom Among the Indians,* for instance, the boys' tales meander; in removing the boys from the confines of the Mississippi valley, Twain removes them from the sphere of their aunts' influence. With no one to rebel against, their pranks lose the energy that creates dramatic tension between the demands of the community and the demands of the individual.

Young women, too, help Twain's protagonists develop moral awareness. Unlike the female authority figures, who tend to disappear in Twain's later works, they are a persistent character type in his writings. They win some of the highest encomiums in Twain's fiction because they not only understand the virtues of selflessness but also act on their principles, often in defiance of current public opinion. Huck, claiming that Mary Jane Wilks is "just full of sand," bases his claim on her moral courage. Not only is the injustice done the Wilkses' slaves enough to ruin her own happiness—she finds herself unable to enjoy the prospect of benefiting personally from the sale of the slaves—she compounds her selflessness by having the courage to pray for Huck. "I reckoned if she knowed me she'd take a job that was more nearer her size," he remarks; nonetheless, he thinks of her "many and many a million times . . . and if ever I'd a thought it would do any good for me to pray for *her*, blamed if I wouldn't a done it or bust" *(HF*, p. 161). Like Jim, Mary Jane teaches Huck to think of other people, especially black people, as worthy of respect; she also teaches Huck to think better of himself for having helped them. Katrina, the servant woman in "No. 44, The Mysterious Stranger," defies the threats of the printers in order to champion the outcast apprentice; while August is too cowardly to act on his own intuitions, she "remained the boy's fearless friend, but she was alone in this" ("No. 44, MS," p. 244). Joan of Arc, of course, acts in defiance of the power structure of France, the English army, and her sex-role and class restrictions, making her "the most noble life that was ever born into this world save only One" *(JA*, 1:xvi). The younger women around whom Twain's men center their affections may be sweet, but they are not passive. They not only say but also do the right thing, generally after the men, morally weaker, have failed.

While older women are mother substitutes in Twain's novels about childhood and unmarried young women are moral exemplars, the woman as a celebrated image did not fully evolve until Twain began transforming his image of Livy into a series of loving wives in his fiction. The clearest—and almost the latest—delineation of the ideal woman in Mark Twain's fiction is the character Eve, from the short sketches "Extracts from Adam's Diary" and "Eve's Diary," finished in 1905, only a year after Livy's death. Like other portions of the "Papers of the Adams Family," these sketches were composed at intervals over a decade or more, but they are printed together in the 1917

Harper's edition of Twain's work, probably because they are so obviously a matched pair in conception and mood. They are unusual in Twain's work in that the diary form permits Twain to portray the woman through her own voice as well as from the male protagonist's or omniscient narrator's point of view. In addition, the two voices permit him to use rhetorical fluidity as an index to the progress of Adam and Eve's relationship. Finally, the diaries are unusual in Twain's fiction because sex is clearly one of the attractions the two humans have for each other.

The theme of "Adam's Diary" and "Eve's Diary" concerns Eve's efforts to make Adam aware that, as another human being, her companionship is necessary for his happiness. Only after he recognizes her significance does Adam become truly human himself. Before he accepts her, his self-image is rooted in his janitorial duties and his self-absorption is reflected in his rhetorical brevity. Twain's strategy for developing their relationship is to show how Adam's control over language expands as he comes to understand how much Eve means to him.

Prior to Eve's appearance in Eden, Adam seems to have regarded himself as a faithful watchman, stolidly—and silently —doing his duty; significantly, he initially resents Eve's chatter because "any new and strange sound intruding itself here upon the solemn hush of these dreaming solitudes offends my ear" ("A&E," p. 343). Much of the charm of these pieces comes from Adam's learning to adjust to the "new creature" in his garden; through the course of his diary he evinces his adjustment by gradually relaxing his language, moving from his initial short, clipped clauses to long, lyrical ones. "This new creature with the long hair is a good deal in the way," he begins. "It is always hanging around and following me about. I don't like this; I am not used to company. I wish it would stay with the other animals" ("A&E," p. 343). Perhaps more than any other of Twain's first-person narrators, Adam is paralyzed by his inability to see the other as subject as well as object; he demonstrates his blindness immediately by referring to Eve as "it" until she teaches him to say "she" and "we."

Eve, however, seeks Adam for companionship; unlike him, she is not happy being alone. He thinks she seeks reflections of herself because she is vain: "she fell in the pond yesterday when she was looking at herself in it, which she is always doing," he sourly remarks ("A&E," p. 346); but she claims to go to the pond "for companionship, some one to look at, some one to talk to. It is not enough . . . but it is something, and something is better than utter loneliness" ("A&E," p. 367). Furthermore, Eve encourages Adam to talk more, surmising that his reticence comes from his conviction that "he is not bright, and is sensitive about it and wishes to conceal it. It is a pity that he should feel so, for brightness is nothing; it is in the heart that the values lie. I wish I could make him understand that a loving good heart is riches . . . and that without it intellect is poverty" ("A&E," p. 367). She encourages his slowly expanding vocabulary, knowing that "it show[s] that he possesses a certain quality of perception. Without a doubt that seed can be made to grow, if cultivated."

Since Adam refuses to acknowledge Eve's right to share his life, she sets herself the immediate task of making him notice that she is not the same as the other animals. Twain illustrates Adam's struggle to reject Eve through his terse sentences, his diction, and his hostility toward her implication that he can no longer think of himself as the only intelligent being around. When Eve first appears Adam notes,

> The new creature says its name is Eve. That is all right, I have no objections. Says it is to call it by, when I want it to come. I said it was superfluous, then. The word evidently raised me in its respect; and indeed it is a large, good word and will bear repetition. It says it is not an It; it is a She. That is probably doubtful; yet it is all one to me; what she is were nothing to me if she would but go by herself and not talk. ("A&E," p. 344)

This passage is significant for the way its language conveys the development of the story's theme. First, Adam's short, choppy sentences convey his unwillingness to engage in conversation with an inferior being; second, he chooses words that will impress Eve with his superiority; third, he insists that Eve's most annoying characteristic is her propensity to talk. Clearly, sound as well as specific words is at issue here, as it is throughout the diaries. Adam resents Eve because she talks; to him; close up; forcing him to answer. Accustomed "only to sounds that are more or less distant from me" ("A&E," p. 343), he resents Eve primarily because she is a sound close to him, one to which he must respond. Adam presents his Eden as a solipsistic universe in which any voice from the outside offends the privacy of his dream; Eve insists that he cease imagining that he is alone and include her in his psychic landscape. One sign of her success is that Adam's smugness is the first indication that he cares that she notices how smart he is.

Adam's emergence from total self-absorption to awareness of the importance of the other is first evident when he realizes that without Eve he would be lonely. After their Fall, Adam suddenly understands that Eve can compensate for the loss of Eden. "I find she is a good deal of a companion," he remarks. "I see I should be lonesome and depressed without her, now that I have lost my property" ("A&E," p. 349). Furthermore, through his association with Eve, Adam learns that the world, even outside the garden, is beautiful. Whereas originally he perceived only objects that were useful to him, he now begins to see objects that stimulate his aesthetic imagination. At once his clauses lengthen; in Twain's mind there seems to be an association between awareness of the significance of others—whether they are other people or simply other aspects of creation—and rhetorical fluidity. Starting with simple adjective-noun combinations—"brown rocks, yellow sand, gray moss"—Adam quickly graduates to metaphor—"the golden islands floating in crimson seas at sunset, the pallid moon sailing through the shredded cloud-rack" ("A&E," p. 373)—language so fluid, especially in contrast to his earlier stop/start sentences, as to indicate a revolution in sensibility. Finally, his appreciation of natural beauty leads Adam to see Eve as the beautiful creature that she is: "Once when she was standing marble-white and sun-drenched on a boulder, with her young head tilted back and her hand shading her eyes, watching the flight of a bird in the sky, I recognized that she was beautiful" ("A&E," p. 373). Having made this leap, Adam suddenly becomes a fully human being, not only knowing that Eve is necessary for companionship but desiring her sexually as well. She, always more ready to articulate her emotions, explicitly attributes her attraction to Adam to his sex. "I love him with all the strength of my passionate nature," she records ("A&E," p. 378). "Merely because he is masculine, I think" ("A&E," p. 380). At the end of his own diary, his language thoroughly relaxed, Adam confesses, "It is better to live outside the Garden with her than inside it without her" ("A&E," p. 356), testimony to the power of sexual companionship to overcome the delights of solitude. While she notes, "I am the first wife; and in the last I shall be repeated," he, at her grave, knows that "wheresoever she was, *there* was Eden" ("A&E," p. 381).

This late piece in many ways summarizes the importance that wives bear in Twain's fiction. Although in many respects Eve simply reflects the popular image of women as being more sociable, more sensitive to the importance of other people, than men, the peculiar twist given that image in Twain's work suggests that for him its significance lay in the woman's power to coax the man out of himself, to make him aware that his is not the only consciousness in existence. As Aunt Polly's efforts to make Tom recognize the vulnerability of others succeed in preparing him to join the community, so Eve's strenuous efforts to make Adam recognize *her* succeed in rescuing him from a solitary paradise that was as sterile as it was ingrown. Twain's "Diaries" are, of course, his version of the fortunate Fall; for all Adam's initial protestations, in retrospect he realizes how lonely it had been to be the only one of his type. Much of his pleasure comes from the fact that with Eve he learns to see aesthetically and to communicate with another being. Within the landscape of his new Eden, she represents the acquisition of truly human emotions and an escape from the paralysis of solitude.

Few of Twain's other late fictional wives have Eve's charm, partly because few are allowed to tell their own stories. Generally wooden, certainly idealized, these characters deserve examination less because they are interesting (on the whole, they are not) than because they reflect the narrators' needs, providing a focus for male emotions that the narrators express in gushing, sentimental terms. As we have already noted, however, sentimental language is one of the means Twain uses to signal the importance of a woman to his characters. Certainly, rhetorical fluidity is an index to Adam's sexual and aesthetic development. Similarly, in Twain's nightmare manuscripts the adulation women evoke indicates the symbolic outlet they offer to men who are often so paralyzed by their troubles or so deeply absorbed in themselves that they have difficulty articulating anything else. Although the women in these stories routinely care for houses and children, their real function is to provide emotional centering for their men. Whether the men accept or reject their women, they are always responding to them; the female figure is often the only secure object in their psychic landscape. One of the objections to Twain's fictional wives always has been that they are stereotypes; unlike the male protagonists, they are rarely allowed to grow and change. But as Carol Christ points out, this is one of the functions of the Angel in Victorian literature; by always being the same, she represents continuity and innocence in a world of flux and corruption.[11] For Twain's protagonists she provides a way to escape not only the anxieties of their public lives but also the anxieties of their private lives.

The woman's status as the guardian of the man's psychic stability is most evident in the "Which Was the Dream?" manuscripts begun in 1896, after Twain's financial collapse and Susy's death, and continued until 1905, shortly after Livy's death. Most of the wives portrayed in these unfinished pieces—especially in the fragments entitled "The Great Dark," "Which Was the Dream?," and "Which Was It?"—are only seen through their husbands' eyes; they are so idealized that it is difficult to consider any of them as bona fide characters rather than as stereotypes. Like Patmore's and Ruskin's Angels, they tend to be enshrined in houses built for them by their men, and within the "vestal temples" they "sweetly rule" by force of their cheerfulness and their moral and mental superiority. In Twain's work, however, the house symbolizes the husband's success as well as the wife's temple. When the husband fails, the house is destroyed. His wife, better able to cope with the loss of her shrine than he with the loss of his reputation, becomes his only reminder of better, "saner" days; if he had regarded her as an Angel before his failure, he regards her as a Goddess afterward. Not only does she continue to present a standard for morality, she also comes to present a standard for reality. As an extension

11. Christ, "Victorian Masculinity." The point, it seems to me, is implicit in Christ's discussion, especially as concerns Tennyson's "isolated maidens."

of her housewifely functions she helps him create order out of the jumble of ideas in his mind; as he becomes more confused he increasingly looks to her to help him know what is real and what is not. If she dies the last vestige of his ability to cope with his environment fails, his self-control dissipates, and he is left lonely, bitter, guilt-ridden, and in doubt about the reality of the nightmare world in which he finds himself.

The "Which Was the Dream?" manuscripts are especially revealing of Twain's conviction that part of a wife's domestic duty is to help her man maintain his reason. Even Alice, of "The Great Dark," is seen by her husband as having "a better head than mine, and a surer instinct in grouping facts and getting their meaning out of them. If I was drifting into dangerous waters now, she would be sure to detect it and as sure to set me right and save me" ("GD," p. 126). Confronted by Henry's insistence that their current life (on a boat sailing endlessly through a sea full of vicious monsters) is a dream and their dream lives the reality, Alice concludes, "I think I know what is the matter. I have been neglecting you for ten days . . . so that I might indulge myself with solitude; and here is the result—you haven't been taking exercise enough" ("GD," p. 133). Alice's response, annoying as it is, nonetheless shows a complex of ideas associated with her role. On the one hand, her answer absolutely trivializes her husband's very real fears. On the other hand, it shows that she knows, from experience, that he has a tendency to become so preoccupied with his thoughts that he does not even take care of himself physically. Despite their many illnesses—or perhaps because of them—many Victorians placed almost as much stress on physical exercise as the current generation, associating a healthy body with a healthy (and pure) mind. In *Nook Farm*, Kenneth R. Andrews notes that favorite outings for the Clemens family and their neighbors included long walks;[12] the entire family, moreover, searched for psychophysical means of curing the many illnesses that plagued them. Exercise was important, if for nothing else than to calm the nervousness and irritability that seemed to plague each member of that family. As one of Twain's many representations of Livy,

12. Kenneth R. Andrews, *Nook Farm: Mark Twain's Hartford Circle*, pp. 94–96. For an excellent review of the issue of physical and mental health in the

Alice's diagnosis of her husband's trouble is based on her experience of Henry's tendency to work off his nervousness imaginatively if he cannot work it off physically. Furthermore, she knows that when he converts excess energies to dreams he generates nightmares. From Alice's point of view Henry's confusion about alternative realities is probably a result of his brooding. After all, she has no subterranean memories of an alternative existence. If her husband thinks this is a dream, the dream is his personal problem, not a collective one.

Also significant in Alice's speech is the fact that she has secluded herself for ten days in order to be alone to grieve over shipmates who had died during their terrible ordeal. In seeking solitude, however, she has clearly forgotten her duties. Men can lock themselves away to grieve or meditate; women must contain their pain and remember that they are always responsible for their families. It is interesting that Henry's "madness" begins when Alice secludes herself; as soon as a wife allows herself to indulge her own desire for solitude her husband's grasp of reality begins to weaken. Henry wants Alice's advice because he trusts her judgment; when she stoutly denies that she has ever lived anywhere but their ship he rapidly doubts himself. In "The Great Dark" the wife is the representative of reason: calming her husband's fears, providing his recreation, and generally coping with domestic life despite the family's situation on a ship going nowhere in a sea full of monsters.

"Which Was It?" and "Which Was the Dream?" have almost identical beginnings: in both a man and wife have agreed to set down the biographies of their families and in both their initial efforts are interrupted by a fire that destroys their house and ruins their lives. The short pieces written by the women demonstrate little but their lack of individuality. Although they are supposed to be beginning with their own autobiographies, they say barely a word about themselves, concentrating instead on their husbands and children. The husbands' autobiographies, in turn, indicate that their wives are the center of their emotional worlds. For instance, Thomas X, of "Which Was the Dream?,"

nineteenth century, see Bruce Haley, *The Healthy Body and Victorian Culture* (Cambridge: Harvard University Press, 1978).

has known and loved his wife, Alison, since their childhoods. In his lyrical introduction to their lives together he illustrates the sanctuary that marriage represented for the busy, upwardly mobile man. "My life began . . . with my marriage," he claims.

> That was my supreme event; that was happiness which made all previous happinesses of little moment; it was so deep and real that it made these others seem shallow and artificial; so gracious and divine that it exposed them as being earthy and poor and common. We two were one. For all functions but the physical, one heart would have answered for us both. Our days were a dream, we lived in a world of enchantment. ("WWD," p. 38)

When he became a prominent man in Washington, Thomas tells us that he "built a costly and beautiful house . . . and furnished it luxuriously" ("WWD," p. 40). Although he acknowledges Alison's dowry as the key to his wealth, he glows in the light of her admiration for his achievements; returning her adoration, he associates her with his home and his happiness.

After fire destroys their house, however, Thomas's business failures, hitherto secret, are exposed. When he realizes that he is not only bankrupt but also dishonored, he apparently attacks one of his accusers, loses consciousness, and remains in a coma for a year and a half. The manuscript breaks off just after he has regained consciousness and is learning that for all her femininity Alison has found work, moved the family into a poor but adequate house, and learned to cope with her difficulties. Despite Thomas's crimes against them—the worst being to black out for eighteen months—Alison has kept the family together, thus not only continuing her maternal role but assuming the paternal one as well, while Thomas has lain in a helpless stupor, one more child to be cared for. Although he is not entirely responsible for his financial debacle, Thomas's poor judgment, coupled with his resort to unconsciousness in the face of his failure, only demonstrates how much weaker he is than his wife.

In "Which Was It?," on the other hand, the fire kills the protagonist's wife and female children as well as destroying the house; their absence precipitates George Harrison's decline into a morass of lies, thievery, and murder. Picking up his section of the family biography fifteen years after the tragedy, he writes in the third person because he cannot bring himself to say "'*I* did such and such things'; it would revolt me, and the pen would refuse" ("WWI," p. 183). In these manuscripts the women are able to survive without the men, but without the influence of women, the men have difficulty keeping mentally or morally afloat.

By insisting that their wives are morally stronger and emotionally stabler than they and that for them marriage is a divine institution, the narrators of the nightmare manuscripts transform their women into minor deities, then turn to them for reassurance when they feel themselves floundering. Even feminine dress and feminine pursuits become signs of the aura of certainty with which men endow their wives. When wives appear in the nightmare manuscripts they are visions of daintiness, complete with ribbons, kittens, party plans, and snuggling children. When Alice comes up from her cabin she wears a wrapper trimmed with lace and carries a basket of pink and gray crewel work with a kitten curled up in it. George Harrison's wife spends the two days prior to her death planning a birthday party for her six-year-old; Alison of "Which Was the Dream?" is in the midst of executing a similar fete when their disaster strikes. These "memorable . . . marvelous days" are ruled by the figure of a woman who, in her care, concern, tranquillity, and creativity, provides a home that the men see as an oasis of contentment in a desert of masculine failures.

That Livy, after thirty years of marriage, still constituted that oasis in Twain's own emotional life is evident from letters as well as fiction written before most of the nightmare manuscripts were begun. In 1895, when the Clemens family was already in "exile" in Europe, Twain reluctantly went to Hartford and visited their house, recently rented out. "Livy Darling," he wrote, "when I arrived in town I did not want to go near the house. . . . But as soon as I entered the front door I was seized with a furious desire to have us all in this house again and right away, and never go outside the grounds any more forever." He compares the ugliness of European interiors to "the perfect taste of this ground floor, with its delicious dream of harmonious color, and its all-pervading spirit of peace and serenity and deep contentment. You did it all, and it speaks of you and praises you eloquently and unceasingly . . . it seemed as if I had burst awake out of a hellish dream, and had never been away, and that you would come drifting down out of those dainty upper regions with the little children tagging after you."[13] Like the wives in the nightmare manuscripts, Livy is the goddess of this house; as with Twain's references to drifting on still water, "peace and serenity and deep contentment" characterize the sphere she rules. House, woman, and children all constitute the "delicious dream" that balances the "hellish" one created by Twain's overconfidence in his financial acumen.

Certainly in *A Connecticut Yankee in King Arthur's Court*, a novel many critics see as embodying Twain's anxieties about the Paige typesetter, Hank Morgan's one period of escape from embattlement occurs during his marriage. Unlike the protagonists of the nightmare manuscripts, Hank does not see himself as a failure, but the rhetorical inconsistencies of the novel make it difficult not to see the ambivalence with which Twain regarded his hero. Hank's hallmark is his aggressiveness; his design is absolute power over the nation, and his response to failure is monomania, insisting that his cadets join him on a clearly suicidal mission. Yet chapter 40, in which he informs us that he has married Sandy, has a different emphasis than any other chapter in the novel. Not only have the brawling knights become united and peaceable, but Hank spends as much time tending to his daughter as he does trying to outwit his rivals; during this brief period his private concerns balance his public ones. Sandy and Hello constitute the only real home he has ever had, and in "the dearest and perfectest comradeship that ever was," Hank discovers a relationship that is clearly his first experience of real intimacy. "People talk about beautiful friendships between two persons of the same sex," he remarks. "What is the best of that sort, as compared with the friendship of man and wife, where the best impulses and highest ideals of both are the same? There is no place for comparison between the two friendships; the one is earthly, the other divine" (*CY*, p. 524). By making marriage a divine relationship, Hank gives himself an alternative to the manipulations that characterize his "earthly" relationships with men. Certainly at the end of the novel, when

13. Dixon Wecter, ed., *The Love Letters of Mark Twain*, p. 312.

he is awakened from his "dream" to find himself separated from Sandy by an abyss of thirteen centuries, he cries out to her to save him from the consequences of his fantasies: "Ah, watch by me, Sandy,—stay be me every moment—*don't* let me go out of my mind again; death is nothing, let it come, but not with those dreams, not with the torture of those hideous dreams!" (*CY*, p. 574). In similar manner, when Twain wrote Livy in 1895 that entering their house made him feel that he had "burst awake out of a hellish dream . . . and that you would come drifting down out of those dainty upper regions with the little children tagging after you," he indicated how central the concept of wife, child, and home was for him as an image of sanity in the midst of chaos. The significance the image held for him intensified as the number of his failures increased; as house, wife, and children disappeared he openly began to question the reality of his waking life.

It is clear to anyone reviewing the history of the Clemens family that Mark Twain's domestic life was often as chaotic as his public one. Sickness plagued the family members, death followed them, visitors invaded their home. Professing to love their Hartford house, they nonetheless abandoned it frequently, either avoiding Hartford's summer fevers by moving to Elmira, a trip that involved an extraordinary amount of baggage, fuss, and stress, or trying to cut down on their extravagance by exiling themselves to a series of hotels in Europe, excursions that involved more moves and financial outlays than would seem worth the effort. Furthermore, having turned Livy into his literary censor, Twain at times resented her prudish standards, and clearly the tensions created by their moves, their social life, their illnesses, their financial ups and downs, and their three young children created a domestic atmosphere that fell far short of the ideal "tranquility and repose" that Twain sought in marriage.

Nevertheless, Mark Twain loved his wife, relying on her to provide him with the guidance he needed more, rather than less, as he aged. "It's mighty hard to hold back [from work] when one is interested," he advised Karl Gerhardt, a young sculptor whom he was supporting, in 1881. "The fact is that one *can't* hold back, but then one's wife must make him do it, when it seems best. That is what one's wife is for, partly."[14] Not only is the woman the sexual and moral other in Twain's mind; she is also the surrogate for his own self-control. Hamlin Hill suggests that Twain's expectation that during Livy's last illness she could continue to soothe him when he embarked on his misanthropic tirades was the reason doctors forbade him access to her sickroom for more than five minutes a day.[15] Certainly soothing overheated male imaginations is one of the functions routinely performed by wives in the nightmare manuscripts, where men rely on women to assure them that they are not going mad.

Shortly before Livy died, Twain—reduced to corresponding with her by letter—quoted from a chapter about women in a standard book on physiology: "Hear Dr. Draper writing about you prophetically," he begins, and then quotes Draper's evaluation of the woman's role:

> But it is in the family and social relations that her beautiful qualities shine forth. At the close of a long life checkered with pleasures and misfortunes, how often does the aged man with emotion confess that, though all the ephemeral acquaintances and attachments of his career have ended in disappointment and alienation, the wife of his youth is still his friend. In a world in which everything else seems to be passing away, her affection alone is unchanged, true to him in sickness as in health, in adversity as in prosperity, true to the hour of death.

Overlooking the fact that this passage is really about men, not women, Twain tells Livy that Draper "knew you well. He knew you accurately, dear old-young sweetheart, he knew you as I know you."[16]

"As I know you." Twain clearly knew Livy on two different levels: the mundane level of communication between two people linked in a common, worldly pursuit, and the idealized level revealed in his letters to her and in the fictional wives that he based on her. When Eve, at the close of her diary, writes, "I am the first wife, and in the last I shall be repeated," she demonstrates through her biblical cadences as well as her words

---

14. Collected Letters, 26 June 1881. Mark Twain Papers, Bancroft Library, University of California, Berkeley, hereafter abbreviated as MTP.

15. Hamlin Hill, *Mark Twain: God's Fool*, p. 56.

16. Sickroom Notes, #27, 31 March 1903, MTP.

Conclusion

8

The Imagination of Escape

On 2 November 1898, Twain wrote to Henry Huddleston Rogers regarding the recent rejection of "My Platonic Sweetheart" from *Harper's Monthly*. Claiming to be glad the short piece had not been accepted, he commented, "Upon a re-reading of it it seems to me to be neither fish, flesh nor fowl." The same day he also thanked Henry Mills Alden, the editor responsible for rejecting it, maintaining, "*I* thought it was good; I think differently, now."[1]

By "neither fish, flesh nor fowl," Twain probably meant that the essay, designed to be a study of his dreams, pointed in too many directions to constitute a clear statement of his intentions. The predominant theme of "My Platonic Sweetheart" does concern dreams; however, the essay also describes an ideal relationship with a perfect woman and nostalgically evokes scenes from Twain's youth. It not only subsumes several of his preferred images under the rubric of dream analysis, it also constitutes Twain's most complete single statement of his belief that he has an alternate, imperishable self, completely separate from his ordinary, mortal self, which is the truly creative part of his being. Furthermore, the essay indicates that he believed his creative other to be native to a universe independent of concrete time. Seen within the context of Twain's quest for an escape from history, the essay stands as his profession of belief in the immortality of his creative self.

Briefly, "My Platonic Sweetheart" is the record of Twain's periodic dream encounters with a mysterious lover. The girl is always fifteen and he is always seventeen, ages Twain apparently thought were presexual, for throughout the piece he stresses that the relationship is platonic. Still, it is intimate: "it

1. Sir John Adams, *Everyman's Psychology*, pp. 202–3. Excerpt in the January

was not the affection of brother and sister—it was closer than that, more clinging, more endearing, more reverent; and it was not the love of sweethearts, for there was no fire in it. It was somewhere between the two, and was finer than either, and more exquisite, more profoundly contenting" ("MPS," p. 287). Here, the ideal relationship between the Angel of the House and her worshiper is raised to an even higher plane: avoiding sexuality, Twain transmutes their attraction into a higher and "finer" kind of love.[2]

In addition to focusing on the ideal woman, the dreams always occur in settings that recall favored periods of Twain's past, locations of natural beauty in which other people are rarely present. He recognizes one of the first as Missouri, where "in front of us was the winding country road, with woods on one side, and on the other a rail fence, with blackberry vines and hazel bushes crowding its angles" ("MPS," p. 288). Another occurs in the Iao valley of Hawaii, "where the drifting scarfs of white mist clove [the mountains] across and left the green summits floating pale and remote, like spectral islands wander-

---

1897 file. Mark Twain Papers, Bancroft Library, University of California, Berkeley, hereafter abbreviated as MTP.

2. If we look at this aspect of "My Platonic Sweetheart" in contrast to a passage from Twain's long notebook analysis of the dreaming and waking selves, we can get an excellent glimpse of both male Victorian schizophrenia about female sexuality and Twain's peculiarly American confusion of race with sexual appetite. The notebook entry for January 1897 is important because it clearly informs all of Twain's later writings about doubles. At the end of his discussion of the Dreaming Self, Twain records a recent dream in which he met a "negro wench" who was "very vivid to me—round black face, shiny black eyes, thick lips, very white & regular teeth showing through her smile. She was about 22, & plump—not fleshy, not fat, merely rounded & plump; & good-natured & not at all bad looking. She had but one garment on . . . She sold me a pie . . . She made a disgusting proposition to me . . . it seemed quite natural that it should come from her . . . I merely made a chaffy remark to brush aside the matter . . . & asked for a spoon to eat my pie with. She . . . took it out of her mouth . . . & offered it to me. My stomach rose" (Unpublished notebook number 32 I, p. 5). The black woman, eating a "hot mushy pie" and propositioning the white man, is the dream antithesis of the Angel: if the white woman cannot provide a focus for sexual desires, the black woman must take her place. Images of blacks and whites express America's schizophrenia generally, and especially on sexual matters, more than any other popular stereotypes, and in recording two racial dream "Sweethearts" Twain reveals his sexual ambivalence as much as he does his racial biases. I think this passage also reveals how superficial Twain's racial liberalism was—his response to sharing a utensil with a black

ing in the deeps of space" ("MPS," p. 297). Once the girl rescues him from a nightmare landscape, materializing in a lecture hall just as he realizes he has no lecture to deliver, and instantly transforming the hall into the Iao valley. Furthermore, the dream landscapes evoke the same tranquillity and peace evoked by Twain's memories of the landscapes of his childhood: "a simple and natural and beautiful world where everything that happened was natural and right." In them he hears "no noise at all; everywhere a Sabbath stillness" ("MPS," p. 291). Finally, the three houses that figure in the dreams are idealizations of houses from Twain's past: first a log house like those from his reminiscences of the Quarles farm or from *Huck Finn*, complete with "the table set and everything on it steaming hot—a roast turkey, corn in the ear, butterbeans . . . —and a cat curled up asleep in a splint-bottomed chair by the fireplace" ("MPS," p. 289); then a variation of Livy's home in Elmira, "a great plantation-house"; finally, a variation on the Clemenses' Hartford residence: "a palatial sort of mansion which was built of red terra-cotta and had a spacious portico, whose roof was supported by a rank of fluted columns" ("MPS," p. 300). Here Agnes, like Alice in "The Great Dark," is crocheting; a sign that in the later stages of Twain's dream the image of the sweetheart began to merge with the image of the wife.

Perhaps even more than its evocation of the ideal woman, the dream sequence fascinated Twain because its episodes occurred independently from the passage of time in his waking life. Not only do the ages of the dream lovers never alter, the time lapses between dreams never disturb them and, most importantly, the time span of the dream seems to have no relationship to the time span of Twain's waking life. After he wakes from one particularly long episode, for instance, he says he "noticed by the clock that I had been asleep less than two minutes. And what was of more consequence, I was twenty-nine years old" ("MPS," p. 294). In addition, the dream language the lovers speak bears the same relation to waking language as dream time to waking time: it is a kind of verbal shorthand or telepathy, conveying complex ideas with an economy of words: "swifter

---

woman reveals how little his subconscious was in tandem with his conscious struggle to have "enlightened" concepts of race.

than waking thought; for thought is not thought at all, but only a vague and formless fog until it is articulated into words" ("MPS," p. 297).

In the dream, time and language are of a different order than they are in the everyday world; so, too, are material objects: once "a man-of-war-bird lit on [Agnes's] shoulder . . . it turned into a kitten . . . soon it was a tarantula . . . then a starfish . . . Agnes said it was not worthwhile to try to keep things; there was no stability about them" ("MPS," p. 298). Moreover, despite the fact that Agnes seems to die at the end of each dream sequence, she never seems conscious of it, and the narrator concludes, "It may be that she had often died before, and knew there was nothing lasting about it" ("MPS," p. 301). In the dream world material forms are not stable, time is not sequential, language is not linear, and death is not final. Rather, all seem controlled by the mind that is shaping the dream.

In "My Platonic Sweetheart" Twain calls that mind the "dream-artist." As proof that his creative self is a different being from his waking self, he notes that the dream-artist is "a master in taste and drawing and color and arrangement. . . . In my waking hours, when the inferior artist in me is in command, I cannot draw even the simplest picture with a pencil . . . but my dream-artist can draw anything, and do it perfectly" ("MPS," pp. 301–2). While he presents the artist in visual terms in this example, in others he refers to it as the "mysterious mental magician," whose visits bring him visions of what life could be like in an ideal existence. Because he has studied his dreams for years, making a habit of recording them as soon as he wakes in order "to find out what the source of dreams is, and which of the two or three separate persons inhabiting us is their architect," he concludes that the mental magician is his creative other, and that it alone is immortal. His dreams are proof that "when we die we shall slough off this cheap intellect . . . and go abroad into Dreamland clothed in our real selves, and aggrandized and enriched by the command over the mysterious mental magician who is here not our slave, but only our guest" ("MPS," p. 304).

"My Platonic Sweetheart" concludes with a grand affirmation of the existence of an alternative universe and of the immortality of the dreaming self. "In our dreams," Twain claims, "we do make the journeys we seem to make; we do see the things we seem to see; . . . they [our Dream Selves] are real, not chimeras; and they are immortal and indestructible. They go whither they will; they visit all resorts, all points of interest, even the twinkling suns that wander in the wastes of space. . . . We know this because there is no other place" ("MPS," p. 303). Twain believed that in his afterlife his creative self would be manifested in its full, infinitely variable, potential, transforming material objects at will, communicating in his heart's language, loving and being loved by a perfect woman. In creative immortality the "mental magician," at home among the "twinkling suns," is master even of time and space.

Because it brings images of women, childhood, and space, all preferred images in Twain's writings, together with the suggestion that the dreaming, or creative, self is immortal, "My Platonic Sweetheart" constitutes Twain's most formal statement of belief that he has an ideal alternative life divorced from concrete time. As we have seen, the grammatical scrambling with which images of water, space, and childhood are usually presented in his writings indicates an authorial search for an escape from temporality, while the rhetorical effusions with which the image of the good woman is presented indicate the emotional outlet she represents for a man so absorbed in himself and his problems that he needs periodic assurance that he is not going mad. Twain's preferred images suggest that he envisioned a state of bliss as an easing of self-consciousness, an almost literal "going-out" of his self from himself. In life as he knew it this was impossible; his acute awareness of suffering, both his own and that of others, and his agonized sense of mortal decay made it impossible for him to imagine that he could be at ease while still subject to the human condition. Loss of self could only be effected if he could escape the reminders of his mortality.

"My Platonic Sweetheart" suggests that Twain developed a metaphysics of creative solipsism as a private counterweight to his public profession of belief in materialist determinism. While determinism explains why he suffers in his waking life, creative solipsism explains why he is happy in his artistic or dreaming life. By positing an artist-self that brings him pictures of the other world, he could both explain experiences he had had throughout his life and give himself a means of transcending the human condition.

In order to understand why Twain's intimations of creative immortality were so important to him it is helpful to observe how the notes of hope and affirmation informing essays such as "My Platonic Sweetheart" contrast with the notes of anger and frustration informing his expositions of materialist determinism. *What Is Man?*, for instance, is a quasi-Platonic dialogue in which the major character, an Old Man, expounds the determinist creed that Twain had absorbed from reading popular expositions of Lockean and Benthamite psychology. Twain always tended to underline phrases he considered important; significantly, in *What Is Man?* most of the underlined passages concern men's powerlessness to change their condition or to originate any new idea. *"None but gods have ever had a thought which did not come from the outside,"* proclaims the Old Man. "A man's brain is so constructed that it can *originate nothing whatever.* . . . *It has no command over itself, its owner has no command over it"* (*WM?*, p. 7). In a similar vein, Twain wrote to Sir John Adams, just after Adams's *The Herbartian Psychology Applied to Education,* a work simplifying philosophy and psychology for school masters, appeared in 1897. In his appreciation of Adams's book the American, probably misunderstanding Adams's presentation of Lockean psychology, claims that he, too, had decided that the mind "originates nothing, creates nothing, gathers all its materials from the outside, and weaves them into combination automatically, and without anybody's help."[3]

Few artists, one suspects, care to think of themselves as mere reweavers of used thread. Both Twain's persistent underlinings and loud proclamations indicate that, emotionally, he rejected the doctrine that man originates nothing, even if he thought that he accepted it rationally. Convinced that truly new pictures did come to him, he sought for an explanation of their origin. In a notebook entry of 1897 he maintains that "The Recent Carnival of Crime in Connecticut," written some twenty years earlier, "was an attempt to account for our seem-

3. Reprinted in Adams, *Everyman's Psychology,* pp. 202–3.

ing *duality*—the presence in us of *another person;* not a slave of ours, but [wholly] free and independent, and with a character distinctly its own."[4] For all its thundering, *What Is Man?* does not resolve the question that had plagued Twain for years; ultimately the Old Man confesses that his philosophy cannot account for the soul. *"Which is I and Which is my mind?,"* Twain had asked Sir John Adams. "Are we two or are we one?"[5]

In contrast to the frustration evident in works like *What Is Man?*, the encouragement evident in works like "My Platonic Sweetheart" suggests that Twain concluded that the existence of the dream-self, or dream-artist, resolved the puzzle of his dual nature. The figure takes many forms in his fiction, from the mysterious strangers who, like the man that corrupted Hadleyburg, appear, change the course of the protagonists' lives, and disappear without a trace, to the truth-tellers of the late fiction, who come from some other world to teach the protagonists about their mortal limitations. The latter are important in the evolution of Twain's solipsism because they are the fictionalized manifestations of his conclusion, as he expressed it in his notebook entries of 1898, that "we have a *spiritualized self* that can *detach itself* & go wandering off on affairs of its own . . . now as I take it, my finer self, my [spiritualized] dream self, is merely my ordinary body and mind . . . freed from clogging flesh and become a spiritualized body & mind."[6]

In "My Platonic Sweetheart," the nightmare manuscripts, and other "dream" writings, the common characteristic of Twain's dream-selves is their ability to collapse time and space. "Waking, I move slowly," he records in his notebook, "but in my dreams my unhampered spiritualized body flies to the ends of the earth in a millionth of a second. Seems to—& I believe, does."[7] As we have seen, in "No. 44, The Mysterious Stranger" August's dream-self claims, "We do not know time, we do not know space" ("No. 44, MS," p. 370). Finally, 44, spirit, stranger, and most articulate exponent of Twain's creed, not only can escape temporality—he brings gifts from the future to August

4. Unpublished notebook number 32 I, 7 January 1897–23 August 1898, p. 2. Twain's brackets.
5. Adams, *Everyman's Psychology,* pp. 202–3.
6. Unpublished notebook number 32 I, p. 4, MTP. Twain's brackets.
7. Ibid.

and re-creates events from the past for him—he can also prove that the real cause of human limitations is the human's need to divide time into arbitrary units, thus disassociating himself both from his past and from his future. "You see," 44 complains, "for your race there is such a thing as *time*—you cut it up and measure it; to your race there is a past, a present and a future —out of one and the same thing you make *three*; and to your race there is also such a thing as *distance*—and hang it, you measure *that*, too!" ("No. 44, MS," p. 331).

As a spokesman for Mark Twain, 44's complaint about time is rooted in Twain's understanding that temporality is the framework for causality. Twain's quarrel with materialist determinism concerned not only determinism's implicit denial of the possibility of creativity but also its control over every event in human life. The fact that free choice was impossible greatly disturbed him; his rejection of the Creator/God concentrated on the effects of natural, or "automatic," law, "exact and unvarying Law," which requires "no watching, no correcting, no readjusting, while the eternities endure!" ("LE," p. 12). Having made man "weak . . . characterless . . . [and] cheaply persuadable" (*WM?*, p. 134), this loveless father withdrew, leaving as his only revelation the "Book of Nature," which "tells us distinctly that God cares not one rap for us; nor for any living creature. It tells us that . . . His laws inflict pain & suffering & sorrow, but it does not say that . . . this is done in order that he may get pleasure out of this misery . . . we do not know what the object is. . . . It may be mere indifference."[8] Like many of his contemporaries in the post-Darwinian era, Twain sees God as withdrawn and indifferent to the sufferings of mankind under natural law. In addition, he saw that under automatic law not only does the race in general suffer senselessly but also that the enlightened individual in particular suffers because he realizes that his freedom to originate new ideas is illusory. "The Turning Point of My Life," commissioned by *Harper's Bazaar* in 1910, shows how belief in determinism neutralized Twain's assessment of his own free will. The assignment was to explain which single incident made him decide to become a writer. Criticizing its premise, Twain notes that the incident itself was "only the *last*

8. Ibid., pp. 23–24.

link in a very long chain of turning-points commissioned to produce the cardinal result" (*WM?*, p. 127). As a mortal, bound by automatic law, he is not only subject to disease, decay, and death, he cannot even make his own professional choices.

The dream-artists, however, being subject neither to the flesh nor to time, can live in any era and take whatever form they choose. For them free choice *is* possible because, being mind rather than matter, immortal rather than mortal, and immune to automatic law, they are not subject to cause-and-effect relationships. Rather, as 44 tells August, they can originate; while "man's mind cannot *create*—a god's can, and my race can." Unlike man's poor mental faculty, which "always has to have the *materials* from the *outside*," the dream-artists "need no contributed materials, we *create* them—out of thought. All things that exist were made out of thought—and out of nothing else" ("No. 44, MS," p. 333). This is the reason for the dream-selves' apparent flightiness: because they can create, destroy, and re-create any situation they wish, they do not have to think about the results of what they do. If they do not like the consequences of their acts, they can rub them out and start all over again, for any situation they encounter is merely a product of their own minds.

The subjective theory of reality discernible in the analysis of the dream-selves informs all of Twain's writings concerning time and dreams. His experiments with relative perceptions of time in the nightmare manuscripts, in "Letters from the Earth," and in any other work comparing extraterrestrial to terrestrial time indicate that he believed that temporality was dependent on the mental capacities of the subject. In works like "3,000 Years Among the Microbes" that explore layered temporalities, the protagonists suspect the worlds in which they find themselves to be emanations of their own imaginations. The subjective quality of the adventure is confirmed by the fact that any protagonist who returns from his dreams to his "real" life finds that no matter how long he seems to have spent "away," little or no time has elapsed on the terrestrial clock. As Alice shrewdly guesses in "The Great Dark," if the protagonists think their environment has suddenly changed, their problem is more likely to be psychological than "real."

Furthermore, we know that in Twain's writings the topography of the universe often stands for the topography of his own mind, indicating that he envisioned his consciousness as a single entity roaming in a vast, dark space. In "No. 44, The Mysterious Stranger," when the dream-selves decribe their existence in "general space," they claim to be able "to rush forever at thought-speed" ("No. 44, MS," p. 377), an image joining concepts of outer universes with concepts of inner ones. Analyzing his dreams in order to discover their origins, Twain seems to have decided that mind and space are one and the same. The vast reaches of outer space through which the dream-self flies are the vast reaches of the subject's inner space, a universe immaterial, atemporal, and rich in creative potential.

By locating the dream-artist's universe within his own inner space, Twain resolved the puzzle of his creativity. The link between the dream-artist and the waking one is that both create worlds out of thought. Both imagine a landscape, people it, impose time spans on its events, decide which acts will precipitate turning points in its characters' lives, and revise it until it is satisfactory. Both begin with a shapeless idea and materialize it, the dream-artist through visions, the waking-artist through words. When the dream-artist constructs a world, it spatializes its thought, expanding and elaborating visual details through dreams. Upon waking, however, the dreamer, the human artist, *re*spatializes his dream through the temporal and spatial dimensions of human language, adding past and future, near and far, to the continuing present and consistent presence of the dream. By recording their adventures in their alternative lives, the narrators of the dream manuscripts show that they can capture their other worlds by writing about them. Through narrating they can seize their thoughts (as Twain seized his dreams by recording them as soon as he awoke), bring them into the world of human time, and examine them almost as archaeological artifacts from another world. Thus, written language becomes a mediating agency between inner and outer worlds, and the art of composition becomes a key to unlock the doors separating "imaginary" and "real" universes; the world of the dream-artist and the world of the waking-self.

The notion that written language was the mediator between

the ephemera of the psychic realm and the reality of the physical had intrigued Twain for many years before he began toying with it in his work. Certainly its germ is evident in a letter he wrote to Livy in 1868, reporting a conversation with his new friend, the Reverend Joseph Twichell. Claiming that he could not remember Twichell's exact words, Twain puts Twichell's ideas into his own phrasing, reporting that Twichell said, "we *didn't* always think in words—that our . . . most brilliant thoughts were far beyond our capacity to frame into words . . .—that often a radiant thought-vision lit up our plodding brains with its weird beauty, and vanished instantly to the heaven it surely came from." Twain claims Twichell believed the "thought-vision" would persist beyond the "prison-house" of the flesh, and "the celestial visitants that haunt us now . . . without form and void, will be stately temples of thought."[9]

As subsequent manuscripts suggest, the Reverend Twichell's "thought-visions" became part of Mark Twain's artistic goal to manifest his most lyrical ideas through language. His choice of words suggests that even in 1868 he saw his artistic transformation of thoughts into words as similar to God's transformation of the formless void into the universe through the Word. But Twain's desire to capture the ephemeral "thought-visions"— which by the definition given in the letter were neither of the earth nor of human origin—became associated with other images of freedom from human limitations. Ultimately they merged with his preferred images to become avenues along which the spirit of the waking-artist could travel to reach his interior space, a universe promising the peace that his exterior world could not render. As a mediating agency, language provided Twain with a means of escaping temporality as well as with an explanation of the origin of his creative images. Not only could he materialize his thoughts by embodying them in the spatial and temporal world of language, he could also detach his preferred images from concrete time by stripping them of temporal distinctions. In doing so he could create "eternal moments" that enabled him to briefly share the blissful experiences of his dream-artist.

9. *Mark Twain's Collected Letters*, vol. 1, 1853–1869, edited by Lin Salamo, #229.

Twain's preferred images are his "thought-visions" materialized by language, his intimations of the dream-self's universe. In mortal time, the "thought-vision" flits away; in spiritual or creative time, past and future are unified into one conscious present in which the thought-vision is captured and made to endure as the time frame of a fictional episode. For the subject experiencing it—like the remembrancer of a childhood reverie —that expanded moment, rather than a progression of moments, becomes the only reality. Or, as Twain noted in his journal in 1896, "there is in life only one moment and in eternity only one. It is so brief that it is represented by the flitting of a luminous mote through a thin ray of sunlight . . . visible but a fraction of a second."[10] The preferred image describes one of the "moments" Mark Twain would have liked to be his eternity.

Although Twain conveyed his intimations of another world literarily through his preferred images, he considered that he had had "real" experiences of it as well. Like his determinism, Twain's metaphysics evolved from concerns that he shared with his contemporaries. As Alan Gribben has shown, he had been interested in phrenology since 1855. While phrenological ideas rarely appear as serious motifs in his work, he did retain phrenological terminology; for example, his use of the word *temperament* to describe human nature in "What Is Man?" reflects the phrenological division of human types into various combinations of the four temperaments.[11] In *Mediums, and Spirit Rappers, and Roaring Radicals,* Howard Kerr has traced Twain's contacts with spiritualists and shown how he incorporated that popular pseudoreligion, again mostly as burlesque, into his fiction.[12] And, less thoroughly, Martin Ebon has traced Twain's faith in mental telepathy in *They Knew the Unknown.*[13] In addition to Twain's flirtations with these pseudosciences, the entire Clemens family believed in the power of mind over matter, particularly in matters of personal health. One of

10. Unpublished notebook number 32ª I, pp. 2–3, MTP.
11. Alan Gribben, "Mark Twain, Phrenology and the 'Temperaments': A Study of Pseudoscientific Influence."
12. Howard Kerr, *Mediums, and Spirit-Rappers, and Roaring Radicals: Spiritualism in American Literature, 1850–1900.*
13. Martin Ebon, *They Knew the Unknown.*

the family's favorite anecdotes concerned Jean trying to think herself out of a stomach ache when she was little more than a baby, and Livy herself had been "raised" from a two-year neurasthenic paralysis by a faith healer when she was an adolescent. Susy Clemens's biography of her father even suggests that once she and her father tried to cure their nearsightedness by thinking right.[14] During the 1895 lecture tour around the world, when Clara and Livy accompanied Twain, while Susy and Jean stayed home, Susy and Clara carried on an active correspondence about the possibility that the mind could control the body's ills. Clara, lamenting her own diseases as well as her father's, insisted, "I am perfectly certain the exasperating colds and the carbuncles come from a diseased mind."[15] Although he burlesqued most faith healers in his fiction, and wrote a whole book in an effort to discredit Mary Baker Eddy, Twain's anger at the professionals stemmed less from his skepticism than from his disgust at those who used the doctrines for their own gain.

Certainly the Clemenses were not alone in these interests, nor was Mark Twain alone in his ability to profess simultaneous belief in determinism and in the mind cure. The nineteenth century saw a rebirth of interest in psychic phenomena at the same time that it saw a rediscovery of determinism through Social Darwinism; the widespread interest in spiritualism, mesmerism, and the like suggests a reaction to the hopelessness of deterministic ideas. Clearly Twain was not the only individual to hope that something existed beyond the harsh, materialist world of the determinists.[16]

As we know, Twain himself was most interested in mental

14. In *Mark Twain: A Biography*, Albert Bigelow Paine quotes Susy's account of both Jean's attempt at self-healing and her attempt, with her father, to cure nearsightedness (2: 842–43). The Jean incident is echoed in several family letters in subsequent years. Hill, in *God's Fool*, p. 52, refers to Livy's being healed.

15. Clara Clemens to Sam Clemens, 7 February 1896, MTP.

16. While both Sholom Kahn, in *Mark Twain's Mysterious Stranger: A Study of the Manuscript Texts*, and William R. Macnaughton, in *Mark Twain's Last Years as a Writer*, touch briefly on similar ideas, Ruth Salvaggio, in "Twain's Later Phase Reconsidered: Duality and the Mind," addresses them directly. Salvaggio thoughtfully examines Twain's attempts to come to grips with his own duality and to examine the workings of the independent mind throughout the *Mysterious Stranger* manuscripts and concludes that although Twain could not work his way out of his duality, he did come to see that the way out of

telepathy (which he called telegraphy). His autobiography records his one major experience of premonition when, as a riverboat pilot, he dreamed about his brother Henry's death, an event that took place a few days later in ways that reflected the details of the dream. This incident may have first fueled his interest in extrasensory perception; notebooks from the 1870s on contain references to subsequent telepathic experiences. One of his later theories held that a letter in the neighborhood of (but not yet delivered to) its recipient could communicate its proximity (and sometimes its subject matter), which explained why letters so often crossed in the mail. In 1882, in a letter to Rutherford Hayes, he noted that Hayes's most recent letter to him had arrived minutes after the family had discussed both mental telegraphy and Hayes's administration, evidence, he thought, that Hayes's letter had influenced their minds. Here he remarks that he had been documenting similar incidents for six years.[17] In 1898 he told Richard Watson Gilder, "Some people do not believe in mental telegraphy, but I have had 21 years of experience of it and have written a novel with that as *motif* (don't be alarmed—I burned it) and I know considerable about it."[18]

In addition to the pseudosciences, Twain was aware of more legitimate forms of exploration into states of mind. Although he admitted to Sir John Adams, "I have never read Locke or any of the many philosophers quoted by you," he did get their ideas secondhand through Adams and the other source books on psychology he read.[19] He also probably read at least parts of William James's *Principles of Psychology*,[20] a work paying

---

determinism was through the potential of the mind that could make contact with the dreaming self.

17. Clemens to Rutherford Hayes, 10 April 1882, MTP.

18. Clemens to Richard Watson Gilder, 6 November 1898, MTP.

19. In *The Herbartian Psychology Applied to Education,* the book Twain read, Sir John Adams goes to great pains to simplify earlier philosophies of knowledge—Plato, Aristotle, Froebel, and Kant, but especially Locke—in order to persuade schoolmasters that they need a theoretical foundation for their profession, and that Herbart's psychology was the most appropriate. Adams is not a dualist, but it is easy to see how Twain, searching for confirmation of his own theories, would read Adams's synopses through the filter of his own ideas.

20. According to Alan Gribben, in December 1892 Clemens's notebook entries suggest that he had bought one of James's books, but it is difficult to tell which. He did list "Prof. Wm. James' psychological bk" as one that he wanted to

serious attention to altered states of consciousness as demonstrated by mesmerists and mediums. Even a casual reading of James's book should suggest contemporary, as well as historical, methods of inquiry into the relationship between conscious and unconscious states. Since thoroughly "legitimate" psychologists were as likely to study mesmerists as schizophrenics, it is not surprising that Mark Twain, whose approach to any field of inquiry was idiosyncratic rather than academic, should give equal weight to a Harvard psychologist and a Rochester spiritualist. He was not the only person to think that such movements and theories were appropriate means of investigating the properties of mind.

A common thread linking telepathy, spiritualism, schizophrenia, and the rest was the assumption that extraordinary psychic phenomena were signs of a universe existing beyond the known universe of linear space and time. The existence of spirits that could communicate from another world, or of alternate personalities that did not know one another, or, especially, of thoughts that could fly instantaneously from one mind to another suggested that the unconscious mind did not have to follow linear, or consecutive, processes, that is, that it was free from the cause-and-effect relationships dictated by automatic law. Furthermore, this hypothesis may have been supported by new technological evidence that it was possible to circumvent ordinary time and space: the telegraph and the telephone were both instruments that could erase temporality and spatiality as mankind had always known them and make instantaneous connections between minds. Popular responses to the X-ray, which enabled men to penetrate to the essence of physical bodies, testify to the fascination the concept generated. Even a writer like Henri Bergson, whose *Time and Free Will* was first published the same year as *A Connecticut Yankee*, sought to fathom the relationship between cognition and the spatial and temporal universe. At the same time that Westerners were conquering their world physically, they seem to have sensed

---

obtain in 1896, and Gribben speculates that he borrowed it from the London Library. Certainly Twain was *aware* of James's work; in a letter to Livy in 1894 he remarked that Elinor Howells "convinced *me*, before she got through, that

that they also might be able to conquer it spiritually, to understand and thus control the unseen, immaterial forces that exist prior to the visible manifestations of physical laws. The first fruits of the electronic revolution suggested that men ultimately might develop the powers of the Gods.

Mark Twain was fascinated by mechanical inventions, especially those that sped the processes of communication. He owned—but could not master—a typewriter, was one of the first residents of Hartford to have a telephone, used the telegraph routinely, went bankrupt supporting a sophisticated typesetting machine, and, significantly, thought of his experiences of extrasensory perception as mental telegraphy. It is more than likely that he regarded telecommunications media as tangible proof that his own experiences of mental phenomena were not unique. If words could speed through space by way of telephone wires, it was more than likely that they could speed through space by way of the ether. All that was missing was the knowledge of how to do it on command.

The complex of ideas created by Twain's forty-year interest in spiritualism, telepathy, psychology, and instantaneous means of communication all stood behind his explorations into the powers of mind, combining with his analysis of dreams as evidence that some part of him was capable of detaching itself from his limited, mortal frame. Certainly telepathy suggests that some aspect of the mind is independent of the body. If a thought from one person can influence the ideas of another without the intermediary of the written or spoken word, it is logical to conclude that there must be something that can be detached from the purely physiological, a metaphysical thinker for whom mechanistic determinism does not account. Since he was already convinced that his dream-self could *"detach itself* & go wandering off on affairs of its own,"* he saw no conflict in the notion that his material body and mind could also project or receive an immaterial thought to or from another material being. Consequently, he considered that he had experienced two types of messages from the immaterial realm: telepathic ones between people, and dream ones between his waking and his dreaming self.

---

she & Wm. J. are right—hypnotism & mind-cure are the same thing" *(Mark Twain's Library: A Reconstruction*, p. 351).

Finally, Twain thought of writing, his craft, as an experience of an altered state of consciousness. For instance, he wrote *Following the Equator* during the months of his most intense mourning after Susy's death, when he says he felt emotionally empty, a "mud image." Nevertheless, he continued to write, claiming to wonder all the while "what it is in me that writes, and that has comedy fancies and finds pleasure in phrasing them. It is a law of our nature, of course, or it wouldn't happen; the thing in me forgets the presence of the mud image and goes its own way wholly unconscious of it and apparently of no kinship with it."[21] Or, as he wrote to Twichell during the same period: "I am working, but it is for the sake of the *work*—the 'surcease of sorrow' that is found there. I work all the days; and trouble vanishes away when I use that magic. This book will not long stand between it and me, now; but that is no matter, I have many unwritten books to fly to for my preservation; the interval between the finishing of this one and the beginning of the next will not be more than an hour, at most."[22] Writing took him away from himself, or allowed his conscious self to be over-whelmed, releasing him from his immediate troubles. By re-trieving the memories of the voyage around the world recorded in his journals and transforming them into a narrative—that is, by creating a linguistic world around them—he obliterated the time that had passed since the voyage ended, letting his creative self take over and make him believe that the narrative was the reality.

In "A Writer's Workshop" Twain compounds references to water, ships, and other selves, all images of escape for him, in speaking of his writing process. "There has never been a time in the past thirty-five years when my literary shipyard hadn't two or more half-finished ships on the ways, neglected and baking in the sun," he begins. "As long as a book would write itself I was a faithful and interested amanuensis . . . but the minute that the book tried to shift to *my* head the labor . . . I put it away and dropped it out of my mind" ("WW," pp. 196–97). Clearly, he did not think of the process of writing as controlled by his waking

---

21. Henry Nash Smith and William M. Gibson, eds., with the assistance of Frederick Anderson, *Mark Twain–Howells Letters: The Correspondence of Samuel L. Clemens and William D. Howells, 1872–1910*, 2: 664–65.
22. Clemens to Joseph Twichell, 19 January 1897, MTP.

self; the books wrote themselves, or another self wrote them for him. When the creative other ran out of material it could not be forced to produce until it had received more. In a frequently quoted metaphor, Twain used another water image to explain the process: "When the tank runs dry you've only to leave it alone and it will fill up again in time—while you are asleep —also while you are at work at other things and are quite unaware that this unconscious and profitable cerebration is going on" ("WW," p. 197). If writing is a process more automatic than willed, and if the mind of the writer is in another temporal realm while he is writing, the creative task must be under the guidance of the dreaming, or creative, self rather than the waking one. Taking over from the "mud image" that is too steeped in its own grief to generate anything, the creative self "has comedy fancies and finds pleasure in phrasing them." It can even re-create moments of repose in the midst of the "mud image's" human agonies, such as the passage describing the journey between Ceylon and Mauritius recorded in *Following the Equator.* Clearly the other self, "wholly unconscious" of the "mud image," unable to feel as Twain feels, capable of creating something out of nothing, is the dream-artist, who "is real, not [a] chimera . . . immortal & indestructible" ("MPS," p. 303).

Perhaps this is one of the reasons Twain was so delighted when he discovered his "systemless system" for dictating his autobiography. As Charles Neider notes in the introduction to his edition of *Mark Twain's Autobiography* (1959), by picking up and putting down topics as he saw fit—that is, by free association—Twain thought he had discovered a "new form and method" of telling his own story, "a form and method whereby the past and the present are constantly brought face to face."[23] Significantly, Twain's new method sounds appropriate for one of his dream-selves: like the atemporal other, during his dictation sessions he flits from topic to topic and time to time. Moreover he reshapes history as he sees fit: "I don't believe these details are right but I don't care a rap. They will do just as well as the facts," he claims.[24] Obliterating elapsed time and

23. Charles Neider, ed., *The Autobiography of Mark Twain* (New York: Harper and Brothers, 1959), p. xii.
24. Ibid., p. xiv.

manipulating his own past, he creates a "historical" past that conforms to his emotional needs. Generating the images himself, but leaving the labor of writing them down—of respatializing them—to his amanuensis, he maintains the illusion that he is actually reliving the past.

Of course, as Sholom Kahn and others have noted, Twain's theories about doubles resemble Freud's theories of the unconscious; Twain's preoccupation with other selves can certainly be seen as part of an introspective tendency observable among many intellectuals in the 1890s and 1910s.[25] Yet Twain's sense of his creative abilities as an emanation from an other over which he had no conscious control is also peculiarly his own. Twain's interest in the creative or dreaming self was longstanding; he used it consciously to explain his own mental processes to others in essays like "In a Writer's Workshop," and he also used it less consciously to create a means of escape from historical circumstance, or necessity, for himself in works like "No. 44, The Mysterious Stranger." Ideally, in a world built out of thought the thinker can manipulate the details of the edifice so that they comply with his spiritual needs. Since the dream-self lives in a realm where tragedy does not exist, clearly it is better to become that alternate self than to remain bound by the "odious flesh." Seeing language as the mediator between inner and outer universes, Twain assigns the writer the task of mastering the connections between language and thought so that by a logical regression he can live in those "stately temples," in the atemporal realm of pure thought rather than in the temporal realm of language and action. When he detemporalizes descriptive passages like the dream-self's vision of home in "general space," or Huck's moments on the river, or his own memories of childhood on his uncle's farm, he materializes a thought-vision and "fixes" it in linear time. Spatializing, or extending, the duration of sensory images by describing them in minute detail, he creates, through words, a verbal "temple" to which both reader and writer can turn for temporary respite from adult human pain.

Yet creating a world out of his own words and moving into it

25. See H. Stuart Hughes, *Consciousness and Society: The Reorientation of European Social Thought, 1890–1930.*

involved as many dangers as it did delights. As Twain discovered when he wrote the ending to "No. 44, The Mysterious Stranger," creative subjectivity could be a trap as well as an escape hatch. Bernard DeVoto long ago enshrined the last chapter of that novel in his essay "The Symbols of Despair," thus triggering a continuing critical argument.[26] In that chapter, we remember, 44 obliterates the universe, leaving August in an "empty and soundless void." Then 44 informs the boy that "nothing exists save empty space—and you!" and that "you are but a *Thought*—a vagrant Thought, a useless Thought, a homeless Thought, wandering forlorn among the empty eternities!" ("No. 44, MS," p. 404–5). Through 44, August achieves what the alienated writer, in his role as creator of fictional worlds, would like to achieve: he has destroyed human history and the created universe and put the teller of the story in God's place. Since the world is "made out of Thought," and since August is "the only existent Thought," any new worlds must be created by him alone.

But this is precisely the problem with Twain's theory of creative solipsism. While 44's command to "dream other dreams, and better!" seems optimistic, the fact is that no work of fiction created by Mark Twain in the preceding ten years—and few works prior to that—had been very much "better" than the rather nasty series of incidents that makes up "No. 44, The Mysterious Stranger." Like Twain's image of his own consciousness, August's mind is envisioned as a light, searching through the vast emptiness of mental space. But August's mind is "by . . . nature . . . inextinguishable, indestructible." Even if he can create and destroy worlds at will, he apparently cannot destroy himself; most importantly, any world he creates will reflect his own limitations. The dream creator, like God, can only construct worlds in his own image, and as August has amply demonstrated, he is "weak, characterless, and cheaply persuadable." Having sought to destroy the entire chain of human history, and to turn the narrator of his tale into a world dreamer, Twain finds that the dreamer himself is intrinsically flawed.

Yet August's vision of solipsistic omniscience is only the ex-

26. Closest to my own position may be E.H. Eby, who, in a reading of the Paine/Duneka version of *The Mysterious Stranger*, also suggests that the theme

treme of Twain's philosophy of creative subjectivity. In "No. 44, The Mysterious Stranger," Twain's narrator assumes personal responsibility for human history only to find that he is trapped in himself, unable to generate anything but reflections of his own consciousness and unable to extinguish his anguished sensibility. In most of Twain's fiction, however, the narrators use their power over the written word to evade human history rather than to rewrite it. For all his philosophical pretensions, Twain's emotional quest was to escape anxiety, guilt, and loneliness rather than to explain them. When his narrators describe places, experiences, or situations that they associate with "peace and contentment and tranquility," they create verbal images that in turn become origins of states of altered consciousness. Images of water and space, reveries of childhood, and even the figure of the good woman and the home with which she is associated are manifestations of thought-visions in words, verbal temples that the narrators construct and to which they retreat for respite in times of stress. Together these images yield a landscape of repose both for the narrators and for the author who has created them, a landscape at once removed from human time and preserved in it through the power of the written word.

Thus, the ability to generate alternative worlds through language becomes the source of spiritual salvation for the artist alienated from his time and for the characters who reflect his anomie. Twain's evocations of childhood are generally seen as reflecting contemporary nostalgia for an irrevocable past,[27] but the grammatical scrambling through which happy childhoods are presented in his work suggests a solution to the problem of alienation that was as much artistic as cultural. In these passages Twain not only looks at the past, he re-creates it, and in confusing past, present, and future tenses, or speaking of his personal past in the present tense, he creates a verbal structure that, by referring to no particular time, exists in any given moment. When Huck finds "home" on the river, he reminds the

---

of creativity, "of art transcending man's limitations," runs through the story. "Mark Twain's Testament."

27. See, especially, Roger B. Salomon, *Twain and the Image of History*, and

reader as well as the writer of the work that during at least one period of our lives we are acutely sensitive of ourselves as part of the cycle of organic continuity. In Twain's work the child who maintains an intimate relation with nature knows that he will never really die. Images of the river are often linked with images of childhood in these passages because for Twain the combination of water and innocence suggested a spiritual state in which he could lose his sense of alienation and feel whole. As the symbol of eternity, the river is the place where the child can escape the fear of death and the moral degeneracy that characterize life on the shore.

From the sensation of floating on the river to the sensation of being becalmed at sea, images of water came to represent a state of contentment and freedom from responsibility for the adult writer. Moreover, as he developed his craft—or, in his own terminology, as he learned to allow his creative self to take possession of his pen—he learned that by reproducing his preferred images in his prose he could make himself believe that he was really there. When, in his *Autobiography,* he claims to be able to "call back" the past, he is evincing more than just a nostalgic vision, he is creating what we have come to call a Proustian moment—letting a single association evoke an emotional and sensory complex that he then immortalizes through language. According to Charles Neider, Twain wrote the Quarles farm section of the *Autobiography* while he was living in Vienna in 1897–1898,[28] the same period during which he was writing "The Man That Corrupted Hadleyburg," *What Is Man?*, the "St. Petersburg Fragment" of the *Mysterious Stranger* manuscripts, part of "The Chronicle of Young Satan," and "My Platonic Sweetheart." Clearly "My Platonic Sweetheart" and the Quarles farm segment provided him with release from the griefs and anxieties that in another mood, he was expressing in those other highly pessimistic, mostly deterministic, works. Rather than revealing his grief about Susy and his frustrations about mankind, in these lyrical pieces he retreated to his private sanctuary, where, dreaming about his childhood or youth, and

---

Tony Tanner, "The Lost America: The Despair of Henry Adams and Mark Twain."

28. Neider, ed., *Autobiography of Mark Twain,* p. x.

obliterating the time that had passed since he last visited the farm, he created a "stately temple" out of words, making it "as real as it ever was, and as blessed." Like Huck's association of one dawn with all dawns, or Twain's many passages describing the ecstasy of being becalmed on the ocean, the act of creating the passage about the child's experiences was the equivalent of being there.

It is not surprising that a writer who could do this—could live in his own stately temples of thought—would come to think of his creative self as inhabiting a universe of its own. Shifting his images of escape from water and childhood to space, in his later life Twain explored the sources of his creativity by seeking contact with the other who directed him when he was composing. Increasingly bitter about the irreversibility of human history, he withdrew to a private exploration of creative omnipotence, only to find that he could not overcome his own limitations. Still, numerous passages depicting a character flying through outer space indicate the ecstasy offered by the suggestion that his mind, released from the restrictions of the flesh, could collapse time and space and live in an eternity of creative freedom. Only through such images could he transcend his hopeless determinism.

With the significant exception of the girl of "My Platonic Sweetheart,"—whose true "Platonism" lies not in her asexuality but in her personal immutability—Twain's ideal women do not represent an escape from temporality. They do, however, represent an area of respite from anxieties generated by historical circumstance, and their importance as idealizations in his fiction bears a direct relationship to the frustrations of his personal life. Happy marriages, like happy childhoods or states of being on water, are regarded as dreams of enchantment, and the women whom Twain's alienated narrators adore figure as goddesses in his landscape of repose, giving their men centers of consciousness in a rapidly deteriorating world. When Twain turned Livy into the Angel of the House in his letters, he created a metaphorical origin for all of his good women. By making her—like Eve—"the first wife, and the last," he created one kind of human being who could endure beyond the corruption of the flesh.

All of these images became emotional metaphors for escape from the human condition for Mark Twain and for the characters who reflect his alienation. Often trying to preserve their integrity in a society with which they are at moral odds, Mark Twain's personae also question their own sanity when they find themselves the only ones in the crowd to perceive as they do. While they frequently resolve their social problems by tricking people into doing what they want, they resolve their spiritual ones by generating images that represent peace and contentment to them, allowing them to forget their alienation by feeling that they are at one with nature or with a sexual complement. In these brief moments of tranquillity the anxiety that marks so many of the works we have examined disappears. No longer fretting about which is "I" and which "Me," or whether the "I" or the "Them" is right, Mark Twain's narrative personae rest in a rare sense of reconciliation. And creating their moments of respite brought Mark Twain into the same landscape inhabited by his questing characters: a realm where women care for him, water bears him away from his responsibilities, children remind him that he, too, has the capacity to be one with nature, and space represents the infinite potential of his creative mind.

Selected Bibliography

A. Primary Mark Twain materials not abbreviated in the text.

Paine, Albert Bigelow, ed. *Mark Twain's Autobiography*. New York: Harper and Brothers, 1912.

———. *Mark Twain's Notebook*. New York: Harper and Brothers, 1935.

Mark Twain's Collected Letters, vol. 1, 1853–1869. Edited by Lin Salamo. Berkeley: University of California Press, forthcoming.

———. vol. 2, 1869–1870. Edited by Frederick Anderson and Hamlin Hill, with the assistance of Dahlia Armon. Berkeley: University of California Press, forthcoming.

———. vol. 3, 1871–1874. Edited by Michael B. Frank. Textual Associate, Kenneth M. Sanderson. Berkeley: University of California Press, forthcoming.

Mark Twain's Notebooks and Journals, vol. 1, 1855–1873. Edited by Frederick Anderson, Michael B. Frank, and Kenneth Sanderson. Berkeley: University of California Press, 1975.

———. vol. 2, 1877–1883. Edited by Frederick Anderson, Lin Salamo, and Bernard L. Stein. Berkeley: University of California, 1975.

———. vol. 3, 1883–1891. Edited by Robert Pack Browning, Michael B. Frank, and Lin Salamo. Berkeley: University of California Press, 1979.

B. Selected Secondary Sources.

Adams, Sir John. *Everyman's Psychology*. New York: Doubleday, Doran, 1929.

———. *The Herbartian Psychology Applied to Education*. Boston: D.C. Heath and Co., 1898.

Andrews, Kenneth R. *Nook Farm: Mark Twain's Hartford Circle*. Seattle: University of Washington Press, 1950.

Bachelard, Gaston. *The Poetics of Reverie: Childhood, Language, and the Cosmos*. Translated by Daniel Russell. Boston: Beacon Press, 1971.

———. *The Poetics of Space*. Trans. Maria Jolas. Boston: Beacon Press, 1969.

Baetzhold, Howard G. *Mark Twain and John Bull: The British Connection*. Bloomington: Indiana University Press, 1970.

Bellamy, Gladys. *Mark Twain as a Literary Artist.* Norman: University of Oklahoma Press, 1950.

Blues, Thomas. *Mark Twain and the Community.* Lexington: The University Press of Kentucky, 1970.

Brodwin, Stanley. "Mark Twain's Masks of Satan: The Final Phase." *American Literature* 45 (May 1973):206–27.

Budd, Louis J. *Mark Twain: Social Philosopher.* Bloomington: Indiana University Press, 1962.

Cable, Mary. *The Little Darlings: A History of Child-Rearing in America.* New York: Charles Scribner's Sons, 1975.

Carrington, George C., Jr. *The Dramatic Unity of Huckleberry Finn.* Columbus: Ohio State University Press, 1976.

Carter, Everett. "The Meaning of *A Connecticut Yankee.*" *American Literature* 50 (November 1978):418–40.

Christ, Carol. "Victorian Masculinity and the Angel in the House." In *A Widening Sphere: Changing Roles of Victorian Women*, edited by Martha Vicinus, pp. 146–62. Bloomington: Indiana University Press, 1977.

Cobb, Edith. "The Ecology of Imagination in Childhood." *Daedalus: Journal of the American Academy of Arts and Sciences* 88 (Summer 1959): 537–48.

———. *The Ecology of Imagination in Childhood.* New York: Columbia University Press, 1977.

Coveney, Peter. *Poor Monkey: The Child in Literature.* London: Salisbury Square, 1957.

Covici, Pascal, Jr. *Mark Twain's Humor: The Image of a World.* Dallas: Southern Methodist University Press, 1962.

Cox, James M. "*A Connecticut Yankee in King Arthur's Court:* The Machinery of Self-Preservation." *Yale Review*, n.s. 50 (1960): 80–102.

———. *Mark Twain: The Fate of Humor.* Princeton: Princeton University Press, 1966.

DeVoto, Bernard. *Mark Twain At Work.* Cambridge: Harvard University Press, 1942.

Douglas, Ann. *The Feminization of American Culture.* New York: Avon Books, 1977.

Ebon, Martin. *They Knew the Unknown.* New York: World Publishing Co., 1971.

Eby, E.H. "Mark Twain's Testament." *Modern Language Quarterly* 23 (September 1962): 254–62.

Eliade, Mircea. *The Myth of the Eternal Return (or, Cosmos and History).* Trans. Willard R. Trask. Princeton: Princeton University Press, 1949.

Fetterley, Judith. "The Sanctioned Rebel." *Studies in the Novel* 3 (Fall 1971): 293–304.

———. "Yankee Showman and Reformer: The Character of Mark Twain's Hank Morgan." *Texas Studies in Language and Literature* 14 (Winter 1973): 667–79.

Foner, Philip S. *Mark Twain Social Critic.* New York: International Publishers, 1958.

Fussell, Edwin. "The Structural Problem of *The Mysterious Stranger.*" *Studies in Philology* 49 (January 1952): 95–104.

Geismar, Maxwell. *Mark Twain: An American Prophet.* Boston: Houghton Mifflin Co., 1970.

Gibson, William M. *The Art of Mark Twain.* New York: Oxford University Press, 1976.

Glick, Wendell. "The Epistemological Theme of *The Mysterious Stranger.*" *Themes and Directions in American Literature,* essays in Honor of Ray B. Browne and Donald Pizer. Lafayette, Ind.: Purdue University Studies, 1969.

Goad, Mary Ellen. *The Image and the Woman in the Life and Writings of MT.* The Emporia State Research Studies, Kansas State Teachers College, vol. 19 Emporia, Kans. 1971.

Gribben, Alan. "'A Splendor of Stars and Sun': Twain as a Reader of Browning's Poems." *Browning Institute Studies* 6 (1978): 87–103.

———. *Mark Twain's Library: A Reconstruction.* 2 vols. Boston: G.K. Hall and Co., 1980.

———. "Mark Twain Phrenology and the 'Temperaments': A Study of Pseudoscientific Influence." *American Quarterly* 24 (March 1972): 45–68.

Guttman, Allen. "Mark Twain's *Connecticut Yankee:* Affirmation of the Vernacular Tradition?" *New England Quarterly* 33 (June 1960): 232–37.

Hansen, Chadwick. "The Once and Future Boss: Mark Twain's Yankee." *Nineteenth Century Fiction* 28 (June 1973): 62–73.

Hill, Hamlin. *Mark Twain: God's Fool.* New York: Harper and Row, 1973.

Houghton, Walter E. *The Victorian Frame of Mind, 1830–1870.* New Haven: Yale University Press, 1957.

Howells, William Dean. "My Mark Twain." In *Literary Friends and Acquaintance: A Personal Retrospect of American Authorship,* edited by David F. Hiatt and Edwin H. Cady. Bloomington: Indiana University Press, 1968.

Hughes, H. Stuart. *Consciousness and Society: The Reorientation of European Social Thought, 1890–1930.* New York: Vintage Books, 1977.

Jensen, Franklin L. *Mark Twain's Comments on Books and Authors.* The Emporia State Research Studies, Kansas State Teachers College, vol. 12. Emporia, Kans., 1964.

Kahn, Sholom J. *Mark Twain's Mysterious Stranger: A Study of the Manuscript Texts.* Columbia: University of Missouri Press, 1978.

Kaplan, Justin. *Mr. Clemens and Mark Twain: A Biography.* New York: Simon and Schuster, 1966.

Kerr, Howard. *Mediums, and Spirit-Rappers, and Roaring Radicals: Spiritualism in American Literature, 1850–1900.* Urbana: University of Illinois Press, 1972.

Kiefer, Monica. *American Children through their Books: 1700–1835.* Philadelphia: University of Pennsylvania Press, 1948.

Lorch, Fred W. "Hawaian Feudalism and Mark Twain's Connecticut Yankee." *American Literature* 30 (March 1958): 50–66.

McLoughlin, William. "The Role of Religion in the Revolution." In *Essays on the American Revolution,* edited by Stephen G. Kurtz and James H. Hutson, pp. 197–255. Chapel Hill: University of North Carolina Press, 1973.

Macnaughton, William R. *Mark Twain's Last Years as a Writer.* Columbia: University of Missouri Press, 1979.

Marx, Leo. "The Pilot and the Passenger: Landscape Conventions and the Style of *Huckleberry Finn.*" *American Literature* 28 (May 1956): 129–46.

Merleau-Ponty, Maurice. "The Child's Relation with Others." *The Primacy of Perception.* Translated by William Cobb. Edited by James M. Edie. Chicago: Northwestern University Press, 1964.

———. *Phenomenology of Perception.* Translated by Colin Smith. New York: The Humanities Press, 1962.

———. "What Is Phenomenology?" In *European Literary Theory and Practice: From Existential Phenomenology to Structuralism,* edited by Vernon W. Gras. New York: Dell Publishing Co., 1973, pp. 69–85.

Miller, J. Hillis. *The Disappearance of God: Five Nineteenth Century Writers.* Cambridge: Harvard University Press, 1963.

———. *The Form of Victorian Fiction.* Notre Dame and London: University of Notre Dame Press, 1968.

Miller, Ruth. "But Laugh or Die: A Comparison of *The Mysterious Stranger* and *Billy Budd.*" *The Literary Half-Yearly* 2 (1970): 25–29.

Paine, Albert Bigelow. *Mark Twain: A Biography.* 3 vols. New York: Harper and Brothers, 1912.

Patmore, Coventry. *Poems.* London: George Bell and Sons, 1906.

Pattison, Robert. *The Child Figure in English Literature.* Athens: University of Georgia Press, 1978.

Pettit, Arthur G. *Mark Twain and the South.* Lexington: University Press of Kentucky, 1974.

Peck, H. Daniel. *A World By Itself: The Pastoral Moment in Cooper's Fiction.* New Haven: Yale University Press, 1977.

Poirier, Richard. *A World Elsewhere: The Place of Style in American Literature.* New York: Oxford University Press, 1966.

Poulet, Georges. *The Interior Distance.* Ann Arbor: Ann Arbor Paperbacks, The University of Michigan Press, 1964.

Regan, Robert. *Unpromising Heroes: Mark Twain and His Characters.* Berkeley: University of California Press, 1966.

Routh, H.V. *Money, Morals and Manners as Revealed in Modern Literature.* London: Ivor Nicholson and Watson, 1935.

Ruskin, John. "Of Queens' Gardens." In *Sesame and Lilies,* pp. 48–79. New York: E. P. Dutton and Co., 1912.

Salomon, Roger B., "Realism as Disinheritance: Twain, Howells, and James." *American Quarterly* 16 (Winter 1964): 532–44.

———.*Twain and the Image of History.* New Haven: Yale University Press, 1961.

Salvaggio, Ruth. "Twain's Later Phase Reconsidered: Duality and the Mind." *American Literary Realism, 1870–1910* 12 (Autumn 1979): 322–29.

Sloane, David E.E. *Mark Twain as a Literary Comedian.* Baton Rouge: Louisiana State University Press, 1979.

Smith, Harold J. *Women in Mark Twain's World.* New York: Carleton Press, 1973.

Smith, Henry Nash. *Democracy and the Novel: Popular Resistance to Classic American Writers.* New York: Oxford University Press, 1978.

———. *Mark Twain: The Development of a Writer.* New York: Atheneum, 1974.

———. *Mark Twain's Fable of Progress: Political and Economic Ideas in A Connecticut Yankee in King Arthur's Court.* New Brunswick, N.J.: Rutgers University Press, 1964.

Smith, Henry Nash, and William M. Gibson, eds., with the assistance of Frederick Anderson. *Mark Twain–Howells Letters: The Correspondence of Samuel L. Clemens and William D. Howells, 1872–1910.* 2 vols. Cambridge: Harvard University Press, 1960.

Spacks, Patricia Meyer. *The Female Imagination.* New York: Avon Books, 1975.

Stone, Albert E., Jr. *The Innocent Eye: Childhood in Mark Twain's Imagination.* New Haven: Yale University Press, 1961.

Strong, Leah A. *Joseph Hopkins Twichell, Mark Twain's Friend and Pastor.* Athens: University of Georgia Press, 1966.

Tanner, Tony. "The Lost America: The Despair of Henry Adams and Mark Twain." *Modern Age* 5 (Summer 1961): 299–310.

Tenny, Thomas Asa. *Mark Twain: A Reference Guide.* Boston: G.K. Hall and Co., 1977.

Tuckey, John S. *Mark Twain and Little Satan: The Writing of The Mysterious Stranger.* West Lafayette, Ind.: Purdue University Studies, 1963.

Wecter, Dixon, ed. *The Love Letters of Mark Twain.* New York: Harper and Brothers, 1949.

———. *Mark Twain to Mrs. Fairbanks.* San Marino, Calif.: Huntington Library, 1949.

Wilson, James D. "In Quest of Redemptive Vision: Mark Twain's *Joan of Arc.*" *Texas Studies in Language and Literature* 20, no. 1 (Spring 1978): 181–98.

Index